Most Excellent Differences

Most Excellent Differences

Essays on Using Type Theory
in the Composition Classroom

Thomas C. Thompson, Editor

Center for Applications of Psychological Type, Inc.

Gainesville, Florida

Published by
Center for Applications of Psychological Type, Inc.
2815 N.W. 13th Street, Suite 401
Gainesville, FL 32609
(352) 375-0160 • (800) 777-2278

CAPT, the CAPT logo, and Center for Applications of Psychological Type are trademarks of Center for Applications of Psychological Type, Inc., Gainesville, FL.

Myers-Briggs Type Indicator and MBTI are registered trademarks of Consulting Psychologists Press, Inc., Palo Alto, CA.

Printed in the United States of America.

ISBN 0-935652-29-9

Library of Congress Cataloging-in-Publication Data

Most excellent differences: essays on using type theory in the composition classroom / edited by Thomas C. Thompson.
     p. cm.
     Includes bibliographical references.
     ISBN 0-935652-29-9
     1. English language—Rhetoric—Study and teaching—Psychological aspects. 2. English language—Composition and exercises—Study and teaching (Secondary)—Psychological aspects. 3. Type theory. 4. Personality. 5. Teacher-student relationships.
6. Learning, Psychology of. I. Thompson, Thomas C. 1958– .
PE1404.M675 1996   96-43373
808'.042'07—dc20   CIP

Table of Contents

Foreword

Every student knows, and almost every teacher has forgotten, that the personality of the teacher is a crucial component of every class. Those of us who teach like to think that we are presenting material rather than ourselves and that our own character is irrelevant to what happens in class. We sometimes imagine ourselves as transparent, as the vehicle through which learning takes place in our students. But if we listen, we can hear our students responding at least as much to who we are as to what we say.

This issue goes beyond the current truism that every teacher is necessarily "situated"—that is, represents a particular sex, age, social class, race, political perspective, religious view, and so on. Some teachers still like to pretend that they are somehow universal characters, altogether neutral on such matters. But this delusion, and it is a delusion, does not remove the fact that they are viewing the material and their students from their own perspectives. Rather it accentuates that fact, since the pretense that it is not there is apparent to everyone except the teacher. Those who fail to recognize their own assumptions are simply in the grip of assumptions they are unwilling to recognize.

But beyond that social and political situatedness lies our own personality, that mysterious complex of responses and behaviors that make us who we are. We are surely also situated inside the persona we put on as children, and that persona has more to do with our teaching than most of us will admit. I think this is true whatever we teach.

But the teacher of writing has a special responsibility and burden in this respect. I remember vividly, almost forty years after the fact, William Perry of the Harvard Bureau of Study Council talking to the teaching assistants beginning composition careers. We were, he told us, on the front lines in relation to students, a kind of early warning system for psychological trouble. We could expect, if numerical predictions held, that one or two of our students might try to commit suicide in the course of the year, and we should keep our eyes out for warning signs. I remember him saying something like this: "You are not trained counselors; you are teachers. But you can save lives by being aware of what your students say in relation to who they are." We were, he continued, the only ones likely to pick up signs of impending disaster, since we were reading weekly what the students were thinking and saying. If we could take a troubled student by the hand and walk him to the counseling center, we could save lives—but that depended on our willingness to adopt a new and strange role, one not comfortable for some of us.

Composition teaching, more than any other university activity, calls for an intersection between the teacher and the student. Consider, for example, the complexity of responding to student writing, a matter much debated these days. The vast variety of responding styles among teachers—most of them negative and unproductive—is slowly emerging from the research. In some cases, our responding patterns have to do with simple acceptance of what our teachers did, rather like parents doing to their children whatever was done to them, including child abuse. Sometimes our responding styles are based on composition theories. But usually we respond out of our personality structure, just as we do in other kinds of social intercourse. Nothing is wrong with this, of course—unless we remain unaware of what we are doing and why, and hence remain unaware of the wide range of options we have.

Surprisingly, this issue of personality and the teaching of writing is a relatively new area of study for compositionists, and most of the work so far has focused more on theory than practice. Hence, the authors in this volume examine the practical ways personality preferences can play out in the composition classroom. They address issues I have wondered about for years, but they do so from a new angle—the lens of personality type theory—and they shed new light on the ways personality can affect the teaching and learning of writing.

I confess that I am skeptical of type theory; like Barry Maid in his chapter, I am convinced that no single theory can explain either composition or personality. Further, as Tom Thompson explains in his chapter, type theory does not attempt to explain all the workings of the human psyche; it simply describes how preferences for certain mental processes over others can influence behavior. Still, I am intrigued and fascinated by these attempts to understand the connection between personality and writing. This book opens new ways to think about the relation of who we are to what we do as teachers. No reader will be able to teach in quite the same way after reading this book.

Edward M. White
San Bernardino, California
May 15, 1996

Preface

In *Hamlet*, Osric describes Laertes as "an absolute gentleman, full of most excellent differences" (V.ii.106–7). In this context, differences are positive; they are valued rather than eyed warily. Too often, however, teachers tend to regard different ways of learning and different ways of teaching—different from their own, that is—as suspect, and probably somehow inferior, if not downright wrong-headed.

Personality type theory, as formulated by Carl Jung and further developed by Katharine Briggs and Isabel Myers, offers another perspective. It allows that different views—or different approaches to teaching, or different methods of doing research, or different strategies for writing essays—can be equally valid, though each will have its own particular strengths and weaknesses. Though it doesn't suggest an "anything goes" approach to teaching, type theory does suggest that different teaching strategies will probably appeal to different students; it also suggests that while one strategy might work well for a given student in one context, another strategy might work better for that same student in another context. In particular, it challenges the notion that there is only one "right" way to teach or to learn.

Researchers are finally beginning to catch up to this idea. In the composition classroom, for instance, talk of "the" writing process (which implies a monolithic process that all writers use) has given way to talk of various writing processes. Some textbooks offer a smorgasbord of writing strategies, then suggest that students experiment with these different strategies to discover which ones work best for them in various situations.

The goal of this book is to give teachers a basic introduction to type theory as a way of understanding some of the behaviors they are likely to encounter in the composition classroom, and to provide some practical advice for applying type theory to their classroom practices.

The first three essays address the first part of that goal: to provide an introduction to type theory as it relates to the composition classroom. Chapter One gives a general introduction to the concept of personality preferences, offering some specific examples of how different classroom behaviors might be reflections of different preferences, Chapter Two suggests that different approaches to the teaching of composition tend to favor certain preferences at the expense of others, and Chapter Three uses the concept of preferences to challenge a dominant model of writing development. The remaining essays address the second part of that goal: to provide some practical advice for applying the theory. Chapter Four offers advice on designing writing assignments, Chapter Five explains the potential benefits of getting feedback from a variety of sources on drafts, and Chapter Six shows how teachers' own preferences can influence the ways they respond to student writing. Chapter Seven offers advice for using type concepts to make writing tutorials more successful, Chapter Eight explains how preferences can affect the dynamics of a computer-assisted classroom, and Chapter Nine shows how students' preferences can influence their views of the library and the act of writing a research paper. Finally, Appendix One offers more detailed descriptions of the ways different preferences combine to form recognizable "types," and Appendix Two provides a brief bibliography of additional readings on type and the teaching of composition.

This volume is not intended to be a stand-alone, "how to use type theory" instruction manual. Rather, it is intended to complement many other valuable type resources already available, with a specific focus on applying type theory in the composition classroom.

Thomas C. Thompson
Charleston, SC
May 23, 1996

1   Understanding Personality Preferences and Type Theory

Thomas C. Thompson

The goal of this chapter is to provide a working knowledge of personality preferences and personality type theory. Once you understand the various preferences and how they work, you should be able to take the information explained in subsequent chapters and apply it to your own classroom. The chapter begins with an explanation of the concept of preferences, a potentially confusing concept that is central to an understanding of personality types. I then describe the eight preferences identified by personality type theory, explain how they interact, and discuss some common misunderstandings people have about personality preferences.

The Concept of Personality Preferences

Personality type theory holds there are different (and opposite) ways of doing things, and that people generally choose to act in certain ways—their preferred ways—over others. One way to think about personality preferences is to compare them to right- or left-handedness. Most people seem to have a decided preference for one hand over the other. They are *capable* of using either hand, of course, and can function when circumstances require them to use a certain hand, but they generally *prefer* to use one hand over the other. You can illustrate the difficulties of using a non-preferred process (i.e., the non-preferred hand) for yourself: simply sign your name with your preferred hand, then sign it again with your non-preferred hand. You can get the job done either way, but it's quicker, easier, and of better quality when you do it the "normal" way.

Another way to think about preferences is to consider the analogy of Early Birds and Night Owls. Early Birds do their best work when they get an early start on the day. Night Owls, on the other hand, may go through the motions of working in the morning, but they don't really hit their stride until much later in the day, or even late at night. Given a choice, these Night Owls would start their work day sometime in the afternoon, work late into the evening, and get up in the morning long after the Early Birds have accomplished much of their day's work.

Of course, there's nothing wrong with being an Early Bird or a Night Owl—in fact, society needs both—but the two groups often make fun of each other, each group implying that the other's time schedule is somehow inferior. Early Birds often can't understand why Night Owls have trouble getting started when the sun comes up; if the Owls would simply go to bed at a reasonable hour, they could function like everyone else. Likewise, the Night Owls wonder about the urge to start and finish so early. If a day's work is completed in a day's time, why should it matter what time of day it is accomplished? So members of each group continue to function in their own ways, convinced that their own schedule is the better one, and perhaps thinking the other group is somehow not quite right.

It's important to note that although Night Owls may *prefer* to work in the evenings and may find that they do their best work then, most are still *capable* of working on a regular day schedule. Likewise, the Early Birds don't turn into pumpkins at midnight; they may be able to function quite effectively when working late into the night (at least on occasion), but the reality is that they are more comfortable, more productive, and less fatigued when they can do their work earlier in the day. It's also important to note that not everyone "fits" clearly in one group or the other. Some people may find that doing their best work depends not on the time of day, but on their motivation. Others may find that they have little or no problem adapting to whatever schedule is demanded of them—and they may consider the whole notion of Early Birds and Night Owls to be rather foolish.

So it goes with the concept of personality preferences, the idea that people tend to prefer certain processes, or certain ways of doing things, over others. Some people will find that they are quite adept at doing things one way, but they have extreme difficulty taking the opposite approach. Others may find that they tend to use one process in certain situations, but are actually quite comfortable using the opposite process in other situations. A few may have trouble identifying *any* processes as their preferred ones, and some will simply see the whole concept of preferred processes as nonsensical. Nevertheless, for those who are able to recognize their own preferred ways of functioning and can understand and respect other ways of functioning, personality type theory can offer useful insights into the complexities of human behavior.

Type Theory and the MBTI

Just as the terms Early Bird and Night Owl describe behavioral patterns, personality type theory is based on observations of behavior. The Swiss psychologist Carl Jung, after years of carefully observing patterns of behavior in his patients, developed a "typology" to describe those patterns — a classification matrix involving two opposite but complementary processes on each of three different indices, describing eight (that is, 2x2x2) different combinations of preferences, or eight general "types" of individuals. Though some critics would reduce the typology to a parlor game or equate it with a horoscope, Jung insisted that it was "far rather a critical apparatus serving to sort out and organize the welter of empirical material, but not in any sense to stick labels on people at first sight" (xiv). That is, his typology simply provided a framework within which to describe and discuss behavioral tendencies; it did *not* purport to reveal the secrets of anyone's psyche based on a classification in one category or another.

While Jung was developing his typology on one side of the Atlantic, Katharine Briggs was developing a similar framework on the other side of the ocean. When Jung's *Psychological Types* was published in English, Briggs recognized Jung's work as a more detailed exposition of her own ideas, so she set out to master the theory as Jung expressed it. She eventually identified a fourth scale she saw implied by Jung's work, though never explicitly described in it, thereby increasing the number of descriptive categories from eight to sixteen.

Later, seeking a way to help people unfamiliar with type theory to identify their own preferences, Briggs and her daughter, Isabel Briggs Myers, developed the Myers-Briggs Type Indicator (MBTI). Early versions of the MBTI were published by Educational Testing Services, and the current forms, which have gone through numerous revisions over the years, are published by Consulting Psychologists Press. The MBTI is available for use only by people with specific training in the use of this or other psychological instruments, but the concepts behind the MBTI are accessible to anyone with an eye for behavioral patterns and a mind open to the idea that perspectives can be in opposition to each other and still both be valid.

Descriptions of the Preferences

Type theory identifies four different personality dimensions, each of which has two complementary (but opposite) preferences, or processes. Those dimensions are orientations toward life (extraversion or introversion), ways to collect information (sensing perception or intuitive perception), ways to make decisions (thinking judgment or feeling judgment), and orientations toward the external world (judging orientation or perceiving orientation). Everyone uses all eight of the processes to some degree, but for each complementary pair, each individual tends to use one process more often, more easily, and with greater skill than the other. That particular process is the *preferred* process, or the *preference* on that particular dimension. What follows is a brief description of the complementary preferences for each of the four scales.

Orientations toward Life: Extraversion and Introversion

The preferences Jung described in greatest detail, and the two generally listed first in discussions of type preferences, are **Extraversion** and **Introversion**, or **E** and **I**. (Jung spelled "extraversion" with an "a," and the spelling stuck.) These preferences describe basic orientations toward life: the extravert habitually focuses on the external world of things, while the introvert usually concentrates on the internal world of ideas.

According to Jung, an extravert is someone whose "whole consciousness looks outward, because the essential and decisive determination always comes from the outside" (334). In other words, when extraverts want to know what's happening, they usually look around, because whatever is important is happening "out there." They may think about those activities later, but they want to check out their surroundings first to have something to think about. That's not to say that extraverts don't ever think, but rather that, given a choice between *doing* something and *think-*

ing about doing something, most extraverts would usually prefer to act.

When introverts want to know what's happening, however, they usually attend first to mental activity rather than to the physical activity around them. It's not that they don't pay attention to things around them, but that they are more interested in monitoring their mental activities than in trying to keep up with the relatively unimportant happenings in the environment. It would also be a mistake to assume that introverts are afraid to act; they would simply rather play out potential actions mentally before deciding whether they actually wanted to follow through with them.

The basic difference between extraversion and introversion is not the *ability* to act on or think about something, but the *preference* to do one or the other first. To an extravert, the outside world is where interesting things happen, so "He who hesitates is lost." To an introvert, however, the hustle and bustle of the outside world can be distracting; the more interesting part of life is the world of thoughts and ideas, so "Look before you leap." Both orientations can be valuable, just as both can be costly, but neither is inherently "better" than the other—they're simply different.

Another way to describe extraversion and introversion is as opposite sources of energy. Extraverts feed on the energy around them, while introverts find energy within themselves. For example, an extravert, after a long and draining day, might want to recharge by socializing with a group of friends—possibly the last thing an introvert in the same situation would want to do. The introvert would probably rather take a solitary walk, or maybe curl up with a good book. Again, that's not to say that extraverts can't stand to be alone, or that introverts are always "wallflowers" at parties. In fact, because extraverts usually spend so much of their time focused outward, they may find their times of solitude to be especially welcome changes, and may value them highly. Likewise, introverts may find short periods of interaction to be quite enjoyable, and a necessary (though relatively small) part of a well-rounded day. In general, however, extraverts like to be engaged with the world around them because they draw on the energy of all that activity, while introverts like to have more time to focus on mental activities.

In the classroom, extraverts are the ones likely to begin working on an assignment before the teacher has finished writing it on the board. They don't typically require much "wait time" when asked a question, because they tend to think *while* they speak rather than *before* they speak. In discussions, they may interrupt frequently, "dumping" their thoughts quickly for consideration. They may have trouble sitting still for long periods of time, such as when listening to a lecture or writing a paper, and they usually work better when allowed to take frequent, active breaks.

Introverts, however, are likely to do well when given long, uninterrupted periods of study. They may even work better when they can get away from the distractions of the classroom. They are less likely than extraverts to contribute frequently to discussions, but when they do say something, it has generally been well thought out. Because they like to rehearse their answers before speaking, they may be slow to respond to questions about new material. Introverts often choose to sit near the edge of the classroom, where they can observe class activities without being caught in the middle of them.

Extraverted teachers are generally more comfortable with noisy classrooms than their introverted counterparts, who like to maintain an atmosphere in which they (and their students) can "hear themselves think." Extraverted teachers also tend to be more activity-oriented, while introverted teachers usually like to allow more time for reflection.

In the general U.S. population, extraverts outnumber introverts, possibly by as much as three to one. That difference may help account for the positive connotations of words that describe extraversion ("friendly," "sociable," "outgoing") and the negative connotations of words that describe introversion ("quiet," "reserved," "shy"). In type theory, however, neither preference is better; each has its own strengths and weaknesses. Extraverts, who are more likely to say whatever happens to be on their mind, may be suspicious of introverts, who appear to be holding something back. For their part, introverts may be annoyed by what they see as excessive (and unnecessary) activity on the part of extraverts.

Ways to Collect Information: Sensing Perception and Intuitive Perception

The next two preferences describe opposite modes of perception, or ways of taking in information: **S**ensing perception and **In**tuitive perception, or S and N. ("Intuitive" is abbreviated with an "N" because "introversion" already claimed the letter "I.") Sensing perception pays attention to discrete bits of information, while intuitive perception (or "intuition") pays attention to the relationship between those bits, or to the picture as a whole. Put another way, sensing perception looks at the trees; intuition looks at the forest.

Sensing perception, as the term implies, refers to the physical senses: taste, touch, sight, sound, and smell. Perceiving with the senses is the act of paying conscious attention to the information provided by those five senses. It is immediate and concrete. Someone using sensing perception pays attention to the particular pieces of information relayed to the brain by the sensory organs, and therefore necessarily attends to the individual parts more than the whole.

Intuitive perception, however, rapidly organizes those discrete pieces of information into meaningful patterns. It focuses less on the data than on the relationships between and among various bits of data. If sensing perception finds meaning in sensory data, intuitive perception creates meaning by assembling the data into patterns.

For example, when the physical senses perceive a knife, fork, spoon, plate, and glass, intuition perceives a place setting. The physical senses perceive several books with the titles "Hamlet," "Macbeth," "Romeo and Juliet," "Julius Caesar," and "Othello"; intuition perceives a set of Shakespearean tragedies. Using sensing perception, a student looks at a poem and counts the lines, voices several lines to determine the meter, and looks at the last word of every line to determine the rhyme before announcing that the poem is an Elizabethan sonnet. Another student, using intuition, sees three quatrains and a couplet, then quickly announces that the poem is a sonnet—of some kind or another.

The sonnet example illustrates another difference between the two kinds of perception: sensing perception is typically slower, but more thorough; intuition is quicker, but often less accurate. Clearly, *some* sensing perception has to occur before intuition can begin to work, but the difference between sensing types and intuitive types is that sensing types attend closely to the sensory information itself, while intuitive types almost immediately begin looking for patterns or other ways to make meaning from that information.

Sensing types like to attend to things they can touch, move, weigh, count, measure, or interact with in other concrete ways. They can add up pieces of information to find larger meanings (as did the student who added lines, meter, and rhyme to identify a sonnet), but the larger meanings are often less interesting or less important than the "hard" data themselves. Intuitive types must pay some attention to their sensory perceptions, but they are generally more interested in using the data to discover or create some kind of whole, and they generally find the whole to be more interesting than simply the sum of its parts.

Still another difference is that sensing types generally enjoy routine; they like to master a skill and perform it over and over. Intuitive types are often quickly bored by routine, and look for new and innovative ways to do things, even if only for the sake of doing them differently. For example, when learning the parts of speech, sensing students are likely to derive satisfaction from working numerous exercises in which they identify the subject and verb in each sentence. Though they may complete all the exercises, intuitive students will probably grow bored or frustrated soon after mastering the concepts of "subject" and "verb." To these students, doing the extra sentences is a waste of time.

As with EI differences, however, SN differences are not absolute. Sensing types are not slaves to routine, nor are intuitive types unable to benefit from it. For example, sensing types might like a change in routine every once in a while, simply for the pleasure of the change. Intuitive types might find it extremely helpful to follow a particular routine, because it lets them operate on "autopilot," leaving their minds free to wander. In general, however, sensing types are more comfortable with routine, while intuitive types gravitate toward innovation.

In the classroom, sensing types are generally drawn more to practice than to theory. Practice is concrete; it's real; it happens in the here-and-now. Practice requires actively engaging the senses. Theory, on the other hand, is abstract; it's hypothetical; it doesn't actually "happen" at all. Theory may require students to engage in mental gymnastics, an activity more appealing to intuitive types. For intuitive types, theory can be fun; they often enjoy playing with ideas just for pleasure. For sensing types, however, theory without application can be a meaningless waste of time.

Sensing students also generally prefer to have precise directions which explain the assignment in detail, and they like to learn material in a step-by-step order. For these reasons, traditional math classes often appeal to sensing types: students learn to add and subtract (which are skills that can be applied in the real world), they practice these skills until they achieve mastery, then they learn to multiply and divide (which build on addition and subtraction), and practice some more. Most new skills build on previously mastered ones, and mathematical laws that work one time, work every time: math is sequential and predictable. For those same reasons, sensing types often find literature classes unappealing: teachers talk about abstractions such as "theme" and "symbolism," and two teachers might have completely different readings of a single text. (How can they *both* be right?) Furthermore, assignments are often vague (such as, "Discuss the theme of this story"), and there's often no single, correct way to respond to an assignment.

The opposite holds true for intuitive students. They like the freedom to respond to assignments creatively. An intuitive student, on being given a straightforward assignment with precise directions, might well ask, "Can I do it my own way instead?" Intuitive types tend to grow bored with step-by-step instruction, so they often begin to look for patterns or short-cuts that will allow them to skip steps and jump ahead. Because they tend to grow bored quickly with detail-oriented work, their work involving details is likely to appear sloppy or inaccurate compared to the work of sensing types.

In the general U.S. population, sensing types outnumber intuitive types the way extraverts outnumber introverts, perhaps by as much as three to one. That ratio might help account for the positive connotations associated with someone who is "practical" and "down-to-earth," and the negative connotations of being a "dreamer" who is "lost in the clouds." In an interesting twist, however, our culture often views intuitive skills as being of a higher order than sensing skills. Part of the reason is that the people who create intelligence tests tend to be intuitive types (who are drawn to the abstract, theoretical world of intelligence-testing). Most intelligence tests are timed, a fact which benefits intuitive types (who read and answer questions quickly) and hurts sensing types (who might read each question several times, and who usually work problems out carefully and thoroughly). Such tests also often measure the ability to work with abstract concepts and hypothetical situations, and to create meanings based on incomplete data—skills which favor intuitive types. Not surprisingly, intuitive types generally score higher on such tests than sensing types, and our culture tends to view "quickness" as an indicator of intelligence.

Ways to Make Decisions: Thinking Judgment and Feeling Judgment

The next preferences describe different kinds of judgment, or ways of making decisions: **Thinking** judgment and **Feeling** judgment, or T and F. Thinking judgment is largely objective; it evaluates data as "true or false," or perhaps "fair or unfair." Feeling judgment is largely subjective; it evaluates data along a continuum from "high value" to "low value." Thinking judgment is more often absolute, while feeling judgment is more often relative. The terms for these two modes of decision-making are perhaps unfortunate, since some people might equate Thinking with Unfeeling and Feeling with Unthinking, neither of which is accurate. The modes might be more accurately captured by the terms Objective and Subjective.

Thinking judgment is objective. People using thinking judgment try to make the decision they see as most fair, even though it might be personally distasteful or might be unpopular for the people affected by it. Thinking judgment tends to place great importance on the objective criteria that relate to a decision, and relatively little importance on the impact of the decision on people.

Feeling judgment, on the other hand, is subjective. That is, people using feeling judgment make decisions in light of their values, and values are inherently subjective. Someone who prefers feeling judgment and who values personal relationships highly might choose an option which, though not necessarily the most fair, manages to maintain harmony in the personal relationships affected by that decision. That's not to say that feeling judgment is emotional or illogical; in fact, both thinking judgment and feeling judgment are rational processes. The difference is simply that thinking judgment uses principles which are absolute, whereas feeling judgment uses value-based criteria which can change according to the specifics of the situation.

To thinking types, feeling judgment can seem inconsistent or mushy; but to feeling types, thinking judgment can seem cold and impersonal. Thinking types generally see themselves as rising above the minor issues that can cloud "clear thinking," and look down on judgment they see as weak or emotional. Feeling types generally see themselves as attentive to the nuances of the immediate situation, and shun judgment they see as shackled by rigid rules which may or may not apply to any particular case. Both kinds of judgment have strengths, but each also has a potential "blind spot."

For thinking types, consistency is a strength. Some teachers, for example, can be especially adept at implementing a grading policy that students see as "tough, but fair," or at applying a set of scoring criteria consistently to a large number of papers. Thinking types are unlikely to spend time trying to decide whether a student has a valid excuse for turning in a paper late, because they probably have a policy of "no excuses; late is late." They are also unlikely to be accused of changing the grading standards from student to student, such as giving a good grade to a mediocre paper simply for "improvement" because the student's earlier papers were especially weak. Thinking types are likely to believe that if grades reflect the quality of the work, then mediocre papers should get only mediocre grades, regardless of any comparisons to other work by the same student.

A potential weakness of thinking types, of course, is that they can fail to consider the "human element" of situations. Teachers who offer criticism in an objective, matter-of-fact way might be perceived by students as thoughtless or even hostile. Students who focus attention solely on the logic of their arguments may overlook both their own ethos and the audience response to their arguments. In short, the danger for thinking types is that they might fail to consider the degree to which subjective responses can affect any transaction between people.

Feeling types tend to be skilled at taking those subjective responses into account. For example, a teacher might be able to use a slightly inflated grade to motivate a student to produce subsequent work that genuinely deserves a high grade; faced with a student's creative but risky response to an assignment, this teacher might soften criticism of an unsuccessful effort as a way to encourage the student to continue to take risks. A student who is skilled at anticipating audience reactions to arguments might be able to produce a persuasive argument even when the "facts" are weak.

The danger for feeling types, then, is that they might focus too much on the audience, ignoring the integrity of their logical arguments. Teachers who prefer feeling judgment might be accused of "coddling" their students, or of being too "touchy-feely" with their instruction. If thinking types are in danger of not attending adequately to students, feeling types are in danger of not attending adequately to student work.

One way to illustrate the strengths and weaknesses of thinking types and feeling types is to compare *Star Trek's* Mr. Spock and Dr. McCoy. Spock, part Vulcan, has almost completely subdued his human side with his Vulcan logic. He is at his best when analyzing data to arrive at logical conclusions, and he is weakest when his human emotions interfere with his logical thought processes. McCoy, on the other hand, views decisions with an eye on the human consequences. He is often infuriated by Spock's excessive objectivity, and Spock in turn finds McCoy's subjectivity annoying. Thinking types and feeling types often view each other's processes with such suspicion.

In the classroom, thinking types often want to know the "why" behind an assignment. If they believe an assignment to be meaningless or irrelevant, they are likely to resist doing it. Once they are convinced that an assignment is reasonable, however, even if they don't like doing the work, they are likely to do it based solely on its merits. In discussions, they can be blunt when stating their views or disagreeing with the views of others, but they can generally produce evidence to back up their claims and opinions. They tend to see issues in black and white, and can be uncomfortable or impatient with multiple "correct" interpretations of a work. They also tend to be concerned with the fairness of class policies, especially grading policies. When writing, they tend to work best with assignments that let them objectively report or analyze information.

Feeling types, however, often need to find a personal connection to a subject to be able to write well about it. Rather than ask, "Is this a good topic?" they tend to ask, "Do I care about this topic?" They are more likely to be motivated by the teacher than by the material, and so are likely to put forth extra effort for a teacher they like, regardless of their particular interest in the material. They are likely to be the peacemakers when discussions get heated, working to maintain harmony by softening pointed views. When opposing viewpoints are voiced, they are likely to emphasize common ground and downplay differences.

In the general U.S. population, thinking types and feeling types appear in roughly equal proportions, though a higher percentage of men are thinking types and a higher percentage of women are feeling types. This distribution may help account for a tendency to label certain characteristics associated with thinking judgment as "masculine" and those associated with feeling judgment as "feminine." Such labeling is unfortunate, because it is often used to dismiss issues rather than to explore them.

Orientations toward the External World: Judging and Perceiving

The final preferences do not appear explicitly in Jung's work; Briggs and Myers saw them as implied by Jung, and made them explicit in the MBTI. They describe different attitudes toward the external world, or different ways of managing one's environment: a **J**udging attitude and a **P**erceiving attitude, or **J** and **P**. A judging attitude is characterized by a tendency to move toward closure. A perceiving attitude is characterized by a tendency to resist closure in order to take in as much information as possible.

Judging types are often goal-oriented. They like to complete projects, whether the project be finishing a task, finding an answer to a question, or simply making a decision. They are apt to make lists of "Things To Do," since they often derive a certain satisfaction from checking off each item as it is completed. To help themselves stay on task and get things done, they tend to be organized, or at least to manage their environment in such a way as to allow them to track their projects until each is completed.

Perceiving types, on the other hand, are often more spontaneous. They tend to be more interested in the ride than the destination. They might make lists, but they rarely look at them afterwards. They are likely to have numerous projects going on at any given time, and are probably more concerned with enjoying a project than with completing it. They like to stay open to new information, and are generally skilled at adapting quickly to unexpected changes of plans.

The strength of a judging attitude is that it leads to closure, but the weakness is that it might lead to closure too quickly. That is, in the quest to draw a conclusion, a judging type might collect only minimal information on which to base that decision; a more thorough preliminary search might turn up data that would lead to a much stronger and better-informed conclusion. Such thoroughness is a strength of a perceiving attitude. A perceiving type is unlikely to reach a hasty conclusion, though the effort to be thorough might cause a failure to reach any conclusion at all.

Another way to look at the difference between judging types and perceiving types is in terms of control. Judging types like to control their surroundings, and perceiving types are generally happy to follow whatever leads the environment provides. Judging types are generally more comfortable with routines, since routines are predictable and generally end with completion. Perceiving types are generally more comfortable with spontaneity; they like to "go with the flow," "roll with the punches," or pursue whatever path seems most interesting at the moment. They aren't concerned about controlling the environment, because they'd rather adapt to whatever situation presents itself.

That's not to say that judging types have an insatiable need to be in control. They simply like to finish what they start, and maintaining a reasonable degree of control over events helps them to stay focused long enough to finish whatever project is underway. Nor is it to say that perceiving types can't manage their own affairs. They simply aren't concerned about focusing on any single project when numerous other projects of equal interest are available to be pursued.

In the classroom, judging types tend to be comfortable with deadlines, and they generally turn in assignments on time. Surprises, such as changing a schedule or interrupting a routine, can be disconcerting to judging types. They generally have good study habits, and when they are allowed to plan their work and follow their plans, their determination can lead them to be overachievers. If they aren't interested in their work, however, they can be in danger of doing "just enough" to get by: just enough research to write the paper, just enough reading to answer the study questions, just enough writing to meet the requirements of the assignments. They might tend to skim material that they should read carefully, and they sometimes draw hasty conclusions based on inadequate information. In discussions, they like to reach closure, and they can be uncomfortable if questions are left unanswered.

Perceiving types tend to be less comfortable with deadlines (which they often see merely as "guidelines"), but they need deadlines to help them complete assignments. In fact, they may work in bursts of energy, enjoying the pressure of racing to meet a deadline. Perceiving types often have fun in class, as they are able to enjoy whatever activity happens to be going on at the moment. They tend to handle the unexpected well, though they can become bored with routines. They might take on too many projects at once, and as a result, might be unable to complete them properly. While they are interested in a project, however, they do quite thorough research on it, even to the point that they generate more information than they can handle. In discussions, they are generally capable of pursuing whatever questions are raised, and they aren't bothered when answers aren't immediately forthcoming. In their writing, they are likely to want to include "everything" on a topic, so they often have difficulty focusing on a single main idea.

In the U.S. population, judging types appear to outnumber perceiving types, but by only a small margin.

Dominant Functions

The concept of preferences suggests that although we use all eight of the processes, we do not use them all with equal frequency or equal facility. The concept of dominant functions suggests that every individual uses one of the perceiving processes (i.e., the processes by which we take in information: sensing or intuition) or one of the judging processes (i.e., the processes by which we make decisions: thinking judgment or feeling judgment) as the central process around which the others are organized. (These four processes are referred to as mental "functions" to differentiate them from the "orientations": E, I, J, and P.) Someone whose dominant function is sensing or intuition has a strong preference for taking in information, with only a secondary interest in using that information to make decisions. Likewise, someone whose dominant function is thinking or feeling is mainly interested in making decisions, with only a secondary interest in gathering information.

Designing instruction to appeal to all of the possible functions is the simplest way to use type theory to make teaching more effective. Creating activities, asking questions, and using assessment measures that allow students to use their dominant functions are ways to let all students draw on their strengths and perform at their best. To illustrate how dominant functions influence the ways teachers assess learning, Elizabeth Murphy divided a group of teachers into four smaller groups according to dominant functions, then asked each group to generate a set of questions to assess student learning on a hypothetical unit on drug awareness (see Chapter 8 in Murphy). The sensing-dominant group asked for specific details of information presented ("Name and describe the major classifications of drugs and their effects on the human body"); the intuition-dominant group asked broad essay questions ("Is the war on drugs succeeding? Why or why not?"); the thinking-dominant group asked questions that appealed to students' powers of logic (Why say no to drugs?"); and the feeling-dominant group asked questions about how drug-related issues affected people personally (How does drug abuse affect the entire family?"). If most of the test questions appealed to a single dominant function (which, of course, would probably be the teacher's dominant function), students for whom that function was less-preferred and less-developed would be at a disadvantage. Including questions that allowed students to draw on the skills associated with all of the functions, however, would give all students equal opportunities to succeed.

Cognitive Orientations

Another way to use type theory in the classroom is to design activities that appeal to the different combinations of perceiving and judging functions, or cognitive orientations. The four possible combinations of these four processes are ST, SF, NF, and NT. Understanding cognitive orientations is slightly more complicated than understanding dominant functions alone, but this understanding gives additional insight into the different ways students view knowledge and process information.

People with an ST orientation tend to take an empirical approach to knowledge. They tend to focus on discrete bits of data and to organize those bits of data logically and impersonally. In the classroom, they tend to view knowledge as absolute and to believe that anything can be understood by breaking it down into its constituent parts. They are probably more comfortable with (and skilled at) identifying the parts of a poem than trying to interpret it, and probably enjoy technical writing more than creative writing.

Those with an SF orientation also attend to the particular, but they tend to view knowledge as more personal than objective. Values play a greater role in the creation of knowledge for SFs, as they are likely to attend to the particulars that matter to them or to some other audience. When writing an essay, for example, SF students are far more likely than ST students to use personal examples to support key points. Just as ST students tend to remain separated from the facts, SF students tend to become involved with them; as writers, they are likely to make a special effort to connect with their audience.

The NF combination is also subjective, as NF students tend to become involved with whatever they are studying, but the focus is on larger patterns rather than particulars. Typically, NF students are more interested in what they see as main ideas than in details, and they generally enjoy possibilities more than realities. They tend to be good at handling abstract concepts, but are usually more interested in knowledge that has practical value than in knowledge for its own sake. For example, NF students would probably rather write a scenario in which Hamlet visits a counselor to discuss his problems than a report on Shakespeare's possible sources for the play.

People with an NT orientation tend to focus on concepts rather than on facts. Unlike NFs, they *do* tend to value knowledge for its own sake, and often enjoy playing with possibilities merely for the sake of argument. In the classroom, they are likely to argue first one side of a position and then the other, letting the logic of the stronger case eventually win out. Like STs, they tend to have strong analytical skills, but tend to apply those skills to broad concepts rather than to discrete bits of information:

NTs would probably rather analyze Coleridge's theoretical differences with Wordsworth than scan a poem.

Personality Types

Dominant functions and cognitive orientations are useful for looking at differences, but the most thorough way to use type theory in the classroom is to develop an understanding of and appreciation for all of the sixteen different combinations of preferences, or "personality types," as illustrated by the "type table" below. In each formula, the dominant process is highlighted for easy reference; the cognitive orientation is identified by the two middle letters.

IS**T**J	IS**F**J	IN**F**J	IN**T**J
IS**T**P	IS**F**P	IN**F**P	IN**T**P
ES**T**P	ES**F**P	EN**F**P	EN**T**P
ES**T**J	ES**F**J	EN**F**J	EN**T**J

Each four-letter combination (or "type formula") offers a shorthand way of listing a person's combination of preferences. Isabel Myers carefully observed the behaviors of people with various combinations of preferences, and based on those observations, she wrote "type descriptions" of people in each category. Of course, no description will completely describe everybody in each category, nor will any individual completely "fit" the description of his or her type. Such descriptions are simply convenient ways to talk about large groups of people who share certain behavioral tendencies. It's important to remember that these descriptions identify tendencies, not laws. Although there are some ways in which you are similar to everyone else who has the same preferences you do, there are other ways in which you are different from all those people. Type theory affirms the uniqueness of individuals while describing certain patterns common to those who have the same preferences. For descriptions of each of the sixteen types, see Appendix 1.

Preferences are not simply additive, but instead interact dynamically. That is, someone who prefers extraversion, sensing, thinking and judging is not simply the sum of E+S+T+J. That's too simplistic a view, both because it fails to consider the ways preferences interact and because it fails to acknowledge that some preferences will be better developed than others. For example, an ESTJ who has well-developed sensing perception but only moderately developed thinking judgment is likely to be quite different from an ESTJ with only moderately developed sensing perception but well-developed thinking judgment. Likewise, the ESTJ who has a strong preference for extraversion will probably behave quite differently from an ESTJ who has only a slight preference for extraversion. Each of the four preferences can be clear or slight, and can be developed to a greater or lesser extent.

Further, an INFP is not the same as an INFJ in terms of I, N and F. Both prefer introversion, so they both tend to look inward at the world of thoughts and ideas, but the INFP looks inward (with feeling judgment) with the goal of making decisions, whereas the INFJ looks inward (with intuitive perception) to consider the ideas without necessarily intending to reach any conclusions. Even though they share three of the four preferences, their behaviors may seem quite different.

If the interactions between preferences seem complicated, that's because they are. That complexity highlights the futility of trying to guess every student's type, as well as the danger of guessing incorrectly (in terms of trying to teach "to" that type). A thorough understanding of type dynamics is not, however, a necessary prerequisite to applying type concepts in the classroom. The utility of knowing *about* personality preferences is in being able to appreciate a variety of approaches to teaching and learning, and in designing classroom activities (from methods of instruction and evaluation to kinds of assignments used) that allow for students with a variety of preferences to draw on their own particular strengths as they learn.

Some Common Misunderstandings

One potential misunderstanding about personality preferences is the assumption that, in a given situation, everybody with the same preference will behave the same way. Such thinking can lead to the kind of labeling Jung warned against and can create or perpetuate unfair stereotypes. The teacher who says, "Because you're an intuitive, you'll probably miss the details of this story," or, "Because you're a thinking type, you probably won't be able to anticipate audience response to your persuasive paper," or even, "Because you're an extravert, you should work well on this collaborative project" is demonstrating poor knowledge of type. Human behavior is far too complex to be explained by type preferences alone, and someone who adopts such simplistic attitudes as those expressed above is likely to do more harm than good to students.

Consider again the analogy of right- and left-handedness. To say that I am "right-handed" is simply to say that I generally write with my right hand: for some reason unknown to me, I preferred to use my right hand as a child, and I have consistently used my right hand more often than my left, so I am more comfortable (and write with greater ease and greater legibility) when writing with my right hand. Manufacturers of school desks know that right-handed people write more easily when the desk top is attached to the right side of the desk, and that the opposite is true for left-handed people, so they wisely make both "right-handed" and "left-handed" desks. School officials, who know that a higher percentage of students are right-handed, generally purchase a higher percentage of right-handed desks for their classrooms. These are examples of people using their knowledge of right- and left-handedness positively.

That knowledge can also be ignored or even abused. The school officials who demand uniformity and purchase *only* right-handed desks create unnecessary hardships for left-handed students. Parents or teachers who force left-handed children to write as if they were right-handed also cause unnecessary problems: the children generally learn to write, but they probably have more trouble doing so, and they may harbor resentment about being forced to function against their natural inclinations.

So it goes with type preferences. Knowing a person's preferences allows me to make certain inferences about the way that person processes information, for example, so I can use that knowledge to communicate with that person more effectively. More importantly, simply knowing that other people *can* function effectively in ways that may seem odd to me should make me more tolerant of those seemingly odd ways of functioning.

Another potential misunderstanding arises from equating a *preference* with a *trait*. A trait is a quality which a person possesses to a certain degree. For example, a measure of traits might produce scores for both "affiliation" and "autonomy." Though these traits seem to be opposites, a person could receive high scores for both; a score for "affiliation" would be completely independent from a score for "autonomy." For any given preference scale on the MBTI, however, a higher score in one direction necessitates a lower score in the other direction. That is, the two preferences on any scale represent opposite ends of a continuum, so a move *toward* one is a move *away from* the other.

For example, consider the act of writing. I might be highly motivated to write, so I might score high on the *trait* "motivation." But when I use that motivation, I do so by picking up a pencil with either my right or left hand—and that choice is influenced by my *preference*. (Even though I might occasionally choose to write with my left hand, or even if I work very hard to develop the ability to write well with my left hand, my natural tendency—my preference—is to use my right hand, so I still describe myself as right-handed.) Further, since I can write with only one hand at a time, I can write at any given moment with *either* my right hand *or* my left, but not both. Especially while I am learning to write, I will probably learn more effectively by using only the preferred hand, even though I do so at the expense of the less-preferred hand. Of course, I can constantly switch from hand to hand in an effort to develop dexterity with both, but the reality is that with such constant switching I will probably fail to achieve competence with either hand. Over the years, as I gain proficiency with one hand, I can begin to work on developing skills with the other hand.

This analogy is also useful for illustrating type development: although developing reasonable skills with less-preferred functions is desirable, there is no need to try to force anyone to develop all functions with equal proficiency. A beginning writer needs to concentrate on learning how to form all the letters; the issue of which hand holds the pencil is irrelevant. The attentive writing teacher will recognize a preference for right- or left-handedness, and will allow the writer to use that hand to move the pencil across the page. The teacher, having had more practice at writing, might actually have learned over the years to write reasonably well with either hand; such a teacher can demonstrate right-handed techniques for right-handed students and left-handed techniques for left-handed students. A competent left-handed teacher, however, can still teach a right-handed student to hold a pencil and form letters legibly. The point is that the teacher doesn't need to demand that all students learn in exactly the same manner.

Type theory holds that people develop proficiency with their various functions by using them over time. Even though preferences don't change, people may develop skills with their less-preferred processes through practice. Most young people, however, have had time to develop only one or two functions well. In a school setting, then, they are probably best served by teachers who allow them to continue to develop proficiency with those preferred functions. Like the novice writer who needs to learn how to write well with the right hand before working with the left hand, the student who prefers sensing perception needs to have opportunities to develop that sensing perception before concentrating too much on developing intuitive perception. Teachers create classrooms in which a variety of students can thrive when they create learning opportunities that draw on the strengths of a variety of preferences.

The chapters that follow offer some additional insights into the ways different preferences can influence classroom behaviors, ranging from the way students approach learning tasks and process new information to the strategies teachers use for presenting information and assessing student learning. They also offer some suggestions for ways you can use your knowledge of type theory to reach more students more effectively.

Work Cited

Jung, Carl G. *Psychological Types*. Trans. H.G. Baynes. Rev. R.F.C. Hull Princeton: Princeton UP, 1971.

Murphy, Elizabeth. *The Developing Child*. Palo Alto, CA: Consulting Psychologists Press, 1992.

2   The Dynamics of
         Teaching and Learning

George H. Jensen and Dean A. Hinnen

Despite the urgings of some of our better thinkers, those who tell us that we must think dialectically, Western civilization still seems to want to split things apart. Consider, for example, our obsession with the nature versus nurture controversy, which surfaces in practically every academic discipline. Even when we encounter thinkers like Jung, who tell us that it is not one or the other but both, we work to simplify his texts. In the case of Jung, our culture has preferred to see him as a psychologist who emphasizes "nature," the influence of instincts. We talk about archetypes as being "intellectual ideas" that are an inborn part of our collective unconscious, ignoring Jung's comments about the cultural and historical influences on the development of archetypes.

In "Archetypes of the Collective Unconscious," as he commented on twentieth-century Europeans' growing fascination with "Asiatic symbols," Jung warned that the archetypes of another culture cannot be adopted wholesale into our own:

> Shall we be able to put on, like a new suit of clothes, ready-made symbols grown on foreign soil, saturated with foreign blood, spoken in a foreign tongue, nourished by a foreign culture, interwoven with foreign history, and so resemble a beggar who wraps himself in kingly raiment, a king who disguises himself as a beggar? (14)

If we try to "cover our own nakedness with the gorgeous trappings of the East," Jung continues, "we would be playing our own history false" (14).

22

As we forget or slight the historical and cultural aspects of archetypes, so too can we view psychological type as transcultural and transhistorical. Jung said in his memoir that he wrote *Psychological Types* to explain how an individual functioned within society (*Memories* 207), and it is precisely this dialectic, the interplay of inborn personality preferences with the temperament of a family or a nation, that permeates Jung's discussion of type.

It is this dialectical view of type theory that we would like to apply to our discussion of teaching and learning styles in composition classrooms. To do so, we will discuss six approaches to the teaching of composition, the evolution of these approaches, and how type is related to each approach. We feel that this is the best way to discuss the subject, because it explains why teachers are often pressured to teach in a way that does not suit their personality types and how students are forced to learn in environments that do not suit their learning styles. To understand what actually happens in composition classrooms, it is necessary to look beyond a teacher's or student's preferred teaching or learning style to the ideology of the profession.

Current-Traditional Rhetoric

When the field of Composition and Rhetoric began to take shape, with the formation of the Conference on College Composition and Communication in 1949, academic life was still under the influence of positivism. To gain credibility, even the soft sciences and the humanities had to make claims to being scientific. During this period, literary critics, most of whom were formalists, created methodologies that critics—all critics, not just the geniuses—could objectively follow to the best interpretation of a text. The then-pervasive methods of teaching composition, based more on lore and hallway adages than research and theory, was what James Berlin has since called Current-Traditional Rhetoric.

Because this approach was pretheoretical (most professors of English felt that the teaching of composition should be left to teaching assistants and the untenured; many high school teachers taught little writing), the practitioners of Current-Traditional Rhetoric did not speak for themselves. Their history has been reconstructed by later composition specialists, almost as if they were archaeologists digging through ruins, even as they sought to dethrone the Current-Traditional approach. As a result, the professional journals contain little in the way of sympathetic accounts. While we will attempt to give this approach its due, it will not be easy. And anything we say that even suggests of sympathy for the approach might be regarded by composition specialists as pure heresy. Nevertheless, the approach and modern theorists' characterization of it both need to be critically reviewed.

It might be argued, with some justification, that writing instruction was minimal—at times, even absent—from Current-Traditional Rhetoric. Often, the instructor lectured out of a grammar handbook or analyzed short stories. When the instructor actually attempted to teach writing, the presentation was usually prescriptive. The instructor pretaught the writing assignment by presenting a list of instructions—often a series of fairly meaningless platitudes or specific prohibitions, such as "use vivid language," "be specific," "no fragments," or "don't use contractions"—and perhaps by specifying a particular organizational format, such as the five-paragraph essay. The students would then write essays on their own, without feedback from the instructor or peers, and submit their work to be graded.

Although this approach might be viewed as highly introverted (introverts are more likely to preteach writing assignments and lecture), we should also acknowledge that the approach was related to a specific ideology. Instructors at this time saw themselves as dispensers of knowledge; the lecture format dominated almost all levels of education. The academy had not yet faced the influx of nontraditional students who would arrive in the mid-1960s, so most instructors felt that students should come to college knowing how to write—even though writing instruction was often supplanted in high school curricula by literature and grammar. "Good writers are born, not taught," the Current-Traditionalist often said. Berlin has gone so far as to say that practitioners of this approach wanted to preserve the status quo, and certainly the emphasis on grammatical correctness (often used to sort out those who were not "college bound" or "college material") supports his claim.

However, amidst this generally ineffective approach were some techniques, since lost to later innovations, that made the writing classroom a more comfortable place for sensing-thinking types (STs) (see Figure 1). The typical practitioner of Current-Traditional Rhetoric gave specific instructions (including her expectations about format and length), broke difficult writing assignments like term papers down into a series of se-

Figure 1. Type and Learning Styles

Extraversion

Es usually learn best in an active environment. They generally prefer to talk through problem-solving and often work best in groups. Es tend to plunge into writing or other activities without much forethought, relying on trial-and-error rather than anticipation to solve problems.

Introversion

Is usually learn best when working quietly and alone. They like to think through problems before talking about them. Is should be given adequate time to formulate their responses during classroom discussions and are more comfortable when they can prepare their responses in advance.

Sensing

Ss prefer the concrete to the abstract and tend to learn best in step-by-step progression. They like clear, specific instructions and are often frustrated when given vague directions. Ss tend to pay attention to details, and usually are better at summarizing material than analyzing it.

Intuition

Ns prefer the abstract to the concrete and can become bored during drills or factual lectures. They thrive in classroom situations that place a premium on imagination, but are sometimes careless about details. Ns tend to be better at analyzing material than summarizing it.

Thinking

Ts tend to make decisions based on logic. They prefer classrooms in which instructors provide a clear rationale for assignments. Ts prefer topics that help them understand systems or cause-and-effect relationships. Ts tend to think syllogistically and analytically.

Feeling

Fs tend to make decisions based on personal values. They prefer assignments in which they can find a human angle or have an emotional invest-ment. Fs are less concerned with logic than with values, and even when their thinking appears syllogistic, it is usually based on personal beliefs.

Judging

Js tend to seek closure. They are comfortable making decisions and once a decision is made they tend to stick to it. Js tend to be well-organized, to meet deadlines, and usually prefer to work on one task at a time. They thrive in a structured classroom environment.

Perceiving

Ps tend to resist closure. They prefer spontaneity and often make decisions only when circumstances require them. Ps like to work on multiple tasks simultaneously and often work right up to—or beyond—deadlines. They thrive in less structured classroom environments.

quenced steps, and clearly laid out what seemed to be definite rules and guidelines. While we are certainly not endorsing a return to Current-Traditional Rhetoric, we do want to validate the complaints that many ST students voice about today's composition classrooms, at least those that are on the cutting edge of more recent theory. These students feel, in general, that instructors who tell them to develop their own topics have abandoned them, that instructors who fail to explain the "steps" to producing a good essay are withholding important information, and that instructors who fail to teach grammar are just not doing their jobs.

Writing as a Process

Around 1965, marked by the publication of D. Gordon Rohman's "Pre-Writing: The Stage of Discovery in the Writing Process," the profession began to move away from "teaching writing as a product" to "teaching writing as a process." Early work in this area was clearly introverted. It focused on "prewriting strategies" — exercises, questions or heuristics designed to help the student develop ideas before writing. The "prewriting strategies," as Rohman saw them, allowed students to think before they wrote; once they developed and clarified their ideas, he believed, the act of putting words on paper would be easy. These strategies work well for most introverted writers, but are less beneficial for extraverts, who prefer to plunge into writing with little planning or to discuss their ideas with classmates rather than to develop them through internal dialogue (see Figure 1).

Soon, however, in the work of Ken Macrorie, Peter Elbow, and Donald Murray, writing teachers offered their students more extraverted advice. They suggested that students talk about their ideas before writing, use freewriting and mapping to leap into writing with little planning, and enter into peer groups to receive oral feedback on their early drafts (see Figure 1).

With the process approach, the act of revision became a crucial component of composition classrooms. While practitioners of Current-Traditional Rhetoric expected students to revise on their own, practitioners of the process approach taught specific revision techniques and provided students with feedback on rough drafts. They also often required students to revise essays after the instructor had written her comments and assigned a grade, often with the possibility of earning a higher grade. The general assumption that revision is good (and the more changes the better) did create difficulties for some students, especially ISTJs and ISFJs, who tend to be one-draft writers. Even with students who tended to be natural revisers (typically FP types), the instructor's admonitions to revise, revise, revise sometimes created a series of drafts that deteriorated rather than improved, or, more seriously, the admonitions sometimes turned a natural reviser into a compulsive, perfectionistic reviser.

Although virtually all of the major studies on the writing process found important individual variations, few textbooks—and, apparently, few instructors—respected these differences. Textbooks and instructors alike discussed the importance of understanding *the* writing process and then went on to describe *one* writing process. We suspect that *the* writing process was often *the* writing process of *the* textbook author or *the* instructor. Such restrictive advice probably helped some students but was perhaps counterproductive for others. This might account for the rather marginal effectiveness of the process approach in Hillocks' meta-analysis of research in the field. The studies of the process approach that Hillocks analyzed were early in its development, and they were not exceptionally sophisticated in their conceptualization of individual differences in writing processes.

While there is certainly a great deal yet to be learned about this approach, that writing should be taught as a process (or processes) is rarely challenged. By 1982, in "The Winds of Change," Hairston used Thomas Kuhn's concept of a paradigm shift in science to suggest—in rather ceremonial rhetoric—that the process approach was firmly established among composition teachers, that something like a Copernican revolution had occurred. Hairston did not discuss one interesting aspect of Kuhn's theory: after a paradigm shift, new knowledge is developed even as "old knowledge," data and ideas that do not easily fit into the new paradigm, is also lost. While composition studies did have a new paradigm (all of the other approaches discussed in this chapter are variations or elaborations on the process approach), an improvement over Current-Traditional Rhetoric, we would also like to suggest that some "old knowledge" was lost, or, to be more precise, a teaching style was lost.

It became unfashionable to be too prescriptive. Students were encouraged to develop their own topics, focus on content rather than mechanics, and revise in a way that showed they had understood rather global (to many students, vague) advice. Sensing types, who were looking for more direction from the teacher, often expressed frustration with the process approach.

Expressivism

The roots of the Expressivist approach are difficult to trace, for one could argue, as many have since Plato, that the use of language is inherently expressive. Much of the basic ideology of the Expressivist approach, however, owes much to Romanticism. As the Romantic movement attacked the rigid attention to form practiced by writers of the Enlightenment (which Romantics saw as chains that bound the human imagination), so too the Expressivists reacted against the scientism of the Current-Traditionalists.

Expressivists, who seem to be predominantly intuitive-feeling types, emphasize the importance of using writing to express emotions, especially in the form of personal narratives; the underlying aim of the approach is to discover the true hidden self as the individual reflects on personal experience. Expressivists tend to prefer writing that is original, that seems to embody the author's voice. Expressivists also tend to view the development of structure as an organic process; structure evolves, they believe, from what the author is trying to say.

This approach to teaching composition developed—or, we could say, underwent reincarnation—almost coterminously with the process approach. Its widespread acceptance among practitioners is due, in part, to its association with the process approach and to its eloquent proponents. Britton and Moffett, two of the widely respected theorists in the field, both present theoretical models that view expressivistic writing as the developmental foundation of other forms of writing. Jensen and DiTiberio (1989) have suggested that such developmental models reflect a type bias: the models assume, in short, that all writers follow the development path of feeling types (see 102–04).

The application of the Expressivist model in theoretical articles, textbooks, and practice has led to its widespread adoption as the foundation of many first-year composition programs as well as the curriculum of many high school English programs. Certainly, all writers can benefit from writing personal narratives, but thinking types often find programs that exclusively assign expressivistic topics extremely difficult. Textbooks or curricula that begin with expressivist topics and move to more "objective" forms of writing, such as argumentation or research papers, can create problems for both feeling and thinking types. At the beginning of the course, when expressivistic writing is emphasized, thinking types tend to struggle while feeling types seem to flourish. Once the shift is made to more "objective" writing, thinking types flourish (apparently improving as writers) and feeling types struggle (apparently deteriorating). Jensen and DiTiberio (1989) offered this basic advice: allow students to begin the semester writing on the kind of topics they find most comfortable; then, as they begin to master that form, encourage them to stretch and grow by moving on to other kinds of topics (see 106–10).

The Cognitivist Approach

The Cognitivist approach, which developed shortly after the Expressivist approach, also built upon the pedagogy of the process approach. Like the Expressivist approach, it focused on the individual writer, but with a major difference. The Cognitivists were not interested in the expression of emotions or the discovery of the hidden self; they were interested in studying, usually with a scientific or quasi-scientific methodology, the decision-making process behind the act of writing. Employing the metaphor of the mind as a computer, Cognitivists sought to gain insight into the way that writers developed ideas, organized essays, and revised. They often asked writers to speak aloud as they wrote (a procedure called protocol analysis), so that their thoughts could be brought out into the open, analyzed, and ultimately explained by a flow chart, the kind of visual diagram of the decision-making process that is often used by computer programmers. As Berlin points out in "Rhetoric and Ideology in the Writing Class," it is a return to the scientism that dominated Current-Traditional ideology (480).

The work of the Cognitivist, which looked at thought processes as if they could be studied apart from emotion or individual differences, seems to reflect a general preference for the thinking function. The application of this theory, say in Linda Flower's textbook, *Problem-Solving Strategies for Writers*, seems well-suited to ST types. After careful study, writing is broken down into discrete tasks that can then be easily translated into specific step-by-step advice. Flow charts abound. For ST types, such an approach makes the complex task of writing seem more manageable.

Now in its fourth edition, Flower's text has undergone significant revision, but its approach to writing still appeals most to introverted, sensing, thinking types. Although Flower now recommends such prewriting heuristics as freewriting, includes a lengthy section on collaborative planning, and addresses both the "cognitive and social view of writing" (vi), her book retains the nine-step, prescriptive approach to writing of its first edition. "The goal of this organization," she explains, "is to introduce the writer, in a systematic way, to distinctive parts of the writing process" (viii). Despite its focus on writing as a process and its updated terminology, Flower's approach still closely resembles that of the Current-Traditionalists, which accounts for its appeal to ST types.

Social Epistemic

In about the mid-1980s, when the Expressivistic approach dominated pedagogy and the Cognitivist approach dominated research, the Social Epistemic approach emerged to challenge both, and, at this time, appears to be the dominant paradigm in composition studies. The Social Epistemic approach seems to have developed from two basic sources: a curriculum for basic writers developed by David Bartholomae and Anthony Petrosky at the University of Pittsburgh and the interest, in a number of disciplines, in social constructionism.

In their book *Facts, Artifacts, and Counterfacts*, Bartholomae and Petrosky describe how they teach basic writing as though they were teaching a graduate seminar. Working with a class of about fifteen students, they integrate reading and writing by moving through a series of texts that are centered around a particular theme; for example, adolescence. As students learn more about the topic—through reading, writing, and class discussions—they begin to see themselves as authorities, as members of a discourse community. Bartholomae and Petrosky argue that, by writing in an "invented" discipline, one that even develops its own vocabulary, students learn what it means to write within the academy. This approach, which emphasizes preparing students for academic writing, very well might embody the academy's bias toward intuition, perhaps more specifically a bias toward the abstract and objective discourse of NT types. It is an approach that seems to work well for preparing students to survive at more demanding institutions.

The second source, social constructionism, is often associated with the work of Lev Vygotsky, although the works of Marx, C.S. Peirce, Clifford

Geertz, Peter Berger, and many others are also often cited. The basic assumption behind social constructionism is that knowledge is socially constructed; it is, in other words, as dependent on ideology, culture, the norms of discourse communities, and methodologies as it is on "truth" or "reality." We have put the terms "truth" and "reality" in quotation marks because they cannot, according to the social constructionist, be known in and of themselves. While this theory can be applied to classrooms without becoming an overt topic of discussion, we would like to point out that it is a theory more easily accepted by intuitives than by sensing types. For sensing types, reality is something that can be touched, smelled, tasted, heard, or seen; it is not an abstract social construction.

These two sources, both of which emphasize the influence of social institutions, naturally grew together and presented a unified attack on Cognitivism and Expressivism. Cognitivism was, in short, criticized for studying the writer in isolation, as if she could write without being influenced by ideology and culture. Expressivism was attacked for not preparing students to write in social situations.

The Environmental Approach

The Environmental approach, which developed in the early 1970s, largely from the work of Lynn Troyka, also acknowledges the social aspects of writing. It does, however, deserve to be distinguished from social constructivism. Rather than have students "invent" their own discourse community, this approach asks students to write within a nonacademic environment. For example, one of the chapters in *Taking Action*, a textbook written by Troyka and Jerrold Nudelman, provides students with background material on a prison riot: pictures and diagrams of the prison facility, the prisoners' schedule, their diet, and other details of prison life. Students then use this rich body of information to play a "simulation game" by assuming one of a variety of roles (warden, prison guard, prisoner, or social worker) in a range of rhetorical situations (for example, a press conference). It seems that sensing types like the details and the concrete situation and that intuitives enjoy thinking about the possibility for change.

As with the epistemic approach, the students build knowledge before writing and assume the role of an authority as they speak or write; however, with the environmental approach, they focus more on nonacademic social interactions than on reading and writing academic texts. It is, as a result, a method that seems to work well for nontraditional students who might be intimidated by academic discourse.

It is also, we should note, an extremely extraverted approach, more naturally suited to extraverted teachers and students. Introverts often find their first simulation games rather stressful and may be reluctant to become as vocal and demonstrative as their extraverted classmates. If not pressured by an extraverted teacher, however, many introverts eventually feel comfortable interacting in this kind of class because they are playing a clear role. They find it easier to adopt the persona of a warden or a prisoner, speaking in another's voice, than they do speaking as "foreigners" in an academic setting. Indeed, students can often find roles that seem well-suited to their personalities.

We should mention that not everyone defines the Environmental approach as we do. Hillocks, in his meta-analysis, says that the approach is characterized by:

1 Clear and specific objectives, e.g., to increase the use of specific detail and figurative language;

2 materials and problems selected to engage students with each other in specifiable processes important to some particular aspect of writing; and

3 activities, such as small-group problem-centered discussions, conducive to high levels of peer interaction concerning specific tasks. (122)

What Hillocks describes and what his example of an Environmental writing assignment shows (123) is an approach that would appeal to both extraverts and sensing-thinking types because it takes the complicated task of writing and breaks it down into "clear and specific objectives" and some step-by-step procedures for achieving those goals. Hillocks' version of the Environmental approach is yet another example of the repackaging of some of the practices of Current-Traditional Rhetoric or a return to ST pedagogy. When discussing the Current-Traditional approach, we said that it has some value (at the risk of labeling ourselves as heretics), especially for ST students. What we have seen is that ST pedagogy returns again and again dressed in new clothes, and for good reasons. Because most of the students in American schools are ST types, a pedagogy fashioned to their needs seems to work. We would only add a qualification: it seems to work well for ST types.

Conclusions

While we have briefly discussed the connection between personality type and teaching style, we do not wish to suggest that this is a causal relationship. Instructors are influenced by their mentors, colleagues, and historical epochs. When Current-Traditional Rhetoric was the dominant approach ("the only game in town"), instructors of all types practiced it and advocated it. We would like to suggest, however, that as alternatives began to develop, the personality types of the innovators did influence the directions those changes took.

Now that instructors are presented with a variety of methodologies, it is easier for them to select an approach that works for them, that draws upon their strengths. They should, however, think about how their approaches might affect some of their students, perhaps students who differ from them in personality type. We would certainly not suggest, however, that instructors must always adapt to the learning styles of their students. This is not only impossible in a classroom setting, it also, as Jung has argued, creates educational monstrosities. (For a discussion of this issue, see Jensen, "Learning Styles," 188–92.) Certainly, an instructor can use an approach and modify it for those students who may feel displaced. An instructor using the environmental approach, for example, could be aware of the difficulty that introverts might have with the approach and be supportive rather than punitive when they are slow to become involved. Instructors can also use individual conferences, responding to essays, and other opportunities to individualize their advice, to teach in a way that makes sense to an individual student.

If instructors are careful to avoid reifying their approach (by saying, "This is how I teach because it is related to who I am"), their students can only benefit. At least then, students will not internalize their discomfort with a certain approach. They will not say, "I am not a good writer." Rather, they will say, "I don't like that approach."

Works Cited

Bartholomae, David, and Anthony Petrosky. *Facts, Artifacts, and Counterfacts: Theory and Method for a Reading and Writing Course.* Upper Montclair, NJ: Boynton/Cook, 1986.

Berlin, James A. "Contemporary Composition: The Major Pedagogical Theories." *College English* 44 (1982): 765–77.

———. "Rhetoric and Ideology in the Writing Class." *College English* 50 (1988): 477–94.

———. *Rhetoric and Reality: Writing Instruction in American Colleges, 1900–1985*. Carbondale: Southern Illinois UP, 1987.

Britton, James. *Language and Learning*. Coral Gables: U of Miami P, 1970.

Elbow, Peter. *Writing without Teachers*. New York: Oxford UP, 1973.

Flower, Linda. *Problem-Solving Strategies for Writers*. 4th ed. Fort Worth: Harcourt, 1993.

Hairston, Maxine. "The Winds of Change: Thomas Kuhn and the Revolution in the Teaching of Writing." *College Composition and Communication* 33 (1982) 76–86.

Hillocks, George, Jr. *Research on Written Composition: New Directions for Teaching*. Urbana, IL: ERIC, 1986.

Jensen, George H. "Learning Styles." *Applications of the Myers-Briggs Type Indicator in Higher Education*. Eds. Judith A. Provost and Scott Anchors. Palo Alto, CA: Consulting Psychologists, 1987. 181–206.

Jensen, George H., and John DiTiberio. *Personality and the Teaching of Composition*. Norwood, NJ: Ablex, 1989.

Jung, Carl G. "Archetypes of the Collective Unconscious." *The Archetypes and the Collective Unconscious*. Trans. R.F.C. Hull. 2nd ed. Princeton: Princeton UP, 1968.

———. *Memories, Dreams, Reflections*. Trans. Aniela Jaffe. New York: Vintage, 1961.

———. *Psychological Types*. Trans. H.G. Baynes. Rev. R.F.C. Hull Princeton: Princeton UP, 1971.

Kuhn, Thomas S. *The Structure of Scientific Revolutions*. 2nd ed. Chicago: U of Chicago P, 1979 (1962).

Macrorie, Ken. *Telling Writing*. 3rd ed. Hasbrouck Heights: Hayden, 1980.

Moffett, James. *Teaching the Universe of Discourse*. Boston: Houghton, 1968.

Murray, Donald M. *A Writer Teaches Writing*. 2nd ed. Boston: Houghton, 1985.

Rohman, D. Gordon. "Pre-Writing: The Stages of Discovery in the Writing Process." *College Composition and Communication* 16 (1965): 106–12.

Troyka, Lynn Quitman, and Jerrold Nudelman. *Taking Action: Writing, Reading, Speaking, and Listening through Simulation Games*. Englewood Cliffs, NJ: Prentice-Hall, 1975.

3　The TF Opposition
　　in Writing Development

Barry Maid

The late 1960s saw a paradigm shift which slowly began to transform Composition Studies. One of the results of this shift has been that composition researchers and teachers have switched from emphasizing the writer's product to emphasizing the writer's process. Along with this change in focus from product to process came a strong commitment to the idea that writing, like other cognitive processes, is inherently developmental in nature. It was, therefore, only natural that much of the research in composition in the early 1970s was directed toward establishing the "Developmental Model" for composing. Researchers like James Britton, Peter Elbow, James Moffet, Janet Emig, James Kinneavy, and others all contributed. What emerged is a universal model, implying that all writers develop through the same pattern. I am, I suspect, always somewhat suspicious of universal models.

Arising from the composing research was the theory that all writers begin by writing "Expressive Discourse" and then develop as writers to write "Transactional Discourse."[1] "Expressive" and "Transactional" are terms that have been used quite frequently by people in Composition Studies for the last twenty or so years, but what still seems to be the best definition appears in James Britton, et. al., *The Development of Writing Abilities (11–18)*. There he says of expressive discourse:

> This is one sense of what we mean by personal: not necessarily that the content of utterance is intimate or private nor that it is actual experience

35

which is being related, but the sense rather that the language and posture of the speaker invites the listener to enter into his world and respond to him as a person. Such language is revealing of self inasmuch as, being informal, and leaving much implicit, it is closer to the way the individual thinks when he thinks by himself than more developed or more mediated utterance. It is this function of language which we have called *expressive*. (141)

Interestingly, Britton goes into depth and uses over one hundred words to describe the expressive function of language. On the other hand, his definition of transactional discourse remains direct and to the point, and it uses only about one third the number of words:

Within the term transactional are classified those uses of language where the writer, operating in a participant role, seeks, in his writing, outcomes in the actual world: to inform or to persuade. (146)

With a clearer idea of what Compositionists mean when they refer to both "Expressive Discourse" and "Transactional Discourse," we can now examine the idea that writers develop skills in expressive discourse before they develop skills in transactional discourse. James Kinneavy's observations in his *A Theory of Discourse* were some of the key factors which led Compositionists to adopt this perspective. There Kinneavy asserts:

As I shall attempt to show, expressive discourse is, in a very important sense, psychologically prior to all the other uses of language. It is the expressive component which gives all discourse a personal significance to the speaker or listener. Indeed, the expressive component of discourse is what involves a man with the world and his fellows to give him his unique brand of humanity. (396)

It was early in the movement of rethinking Composition Studies (1970) that Kinneavy wrote of the value of "Expressive Discourse" in a writer's developmental pattern. His assertion has generally become axiomatic for those who have accepted the new paradigm in Composition Studies. Yet, this theory—that all writers develop from being proficient in expressive discourse to being proficient in transactional discourse—is based on the assumption that all humans develop alike. The assumption that "one developmental model fits all" is, at best, tenuous.

Despite my intuitive knowledge that the new paradigm of writing development didn't always seem to work, I tended to believe it. Indeed, the composition program which I helped to design in the mid-1980s at the University of Arkansas at Little Rock reflects the developmental model that writers will be most comfortable when their first writing experiences are with expressive discourse. Once they have practice and success with expressive discourse, they will then be able to move on (developmentally) to write effective transactional discourse. In our program the first writing course, Composition I, focuses on expressive discourse. The second semester course, Composition II, asks the students, who now have a semester's experience of writing expressive discourse, to write transactional discourse.

Even though our composition program is theoretically sound, I saw results that consistently challenged the theory. Although some students jumped right in during the first semester course and produced wonderful expressive writing, those same students sometimes had real trouble in the second semester. It would have been easy to postulate that they had simply not reached the appropriate stage of writing development to write effective transactional discourse. Further, I also regularly observed another phenomenon. There were large numbers of students who had all kinds of problems in the first semester course. We expected that these student writers, based on the expressive-to-transactional model of writing development, would have even more serious difficulties in the second semester course. More often than not, however, these same weak writers from the first semester became stronger writers in the second semester.

In addition to my observations of students, since I, too, belong to the community of writers, my own feelings regarding my own writing are in direct conflict to the very theory I was espousing. Even now as a writer with years more experience than the typical first-year college student, I find myself uncomfortable with producing expressive discourse. I would much rather write about something other than myself. In addition, when I do write about myself, I am more likely to choose (and am more comfortable in choosing) language which points to the external world. Clearly, something is at work here that is not being explained by current composition theory.

During this same time period as a result of my curiosity with differences in the successful writing processes of student writers as well as differences in successful teaching styles of different instructors, I became interested in type theory. Type theory, quite plainly, allows for and helps to explain the different processes I had been observing over the years.

The work of George H. Jensen and John K. DiTiberio stands as the most significant thinking in the area of personality and writing. Using the pioneering work of Jensen and DiTiberio combined with general type theory, especially as articulated in Myers and Myers' *Gifts Differing* and the Myers and McCaulley's *Manual*, does help to point us in some potentially fruitful directions for understanding the deviation from current composition theory which I was observing in the skills of developing student writers.

My problem, then, was what aspect of type theory would help me to better understand and explain the phenomenon I was observing in my students and in myself as a writer. While fully cognizant that what I was observing might be a function of the EI opposition (since there was clearly a focus on either the inner or outer world), my intuition led me to explore the TF opposition. (I am fully aware that any study of just one of the oppositions defined by type theory is necessarily overly simplistic. Indeed, the EI opposition may act as a confirming or mitigating control over what I am describing.)

The Study

Given the hypothesis that somehow the TF opposition had an impact on a writer's development, I began my study. The writers I looked at were students in the Writing Center and in Composition I classes at the University of Arkansas at Little Rock. In order to avoid the necessity of having to explain the concepts of "expressive" and "transactional," I chose to ask students to respond to writing prompts in either a "personal" or an "analytical" fashion.

At this beginning point I ran into my first difficulty. The graduate assistant working with me on the project (an INFP) felt most strongly that any initial response must necessarily be "personal." Indeed, her response proved to accurately reflect the feelings of the F writers in the sample. In order to better meet her needs, I tried to find another word. In the end, however, I discovered that F types generally felt uncomfortable with any word that I tried. I reluctantly went back to "analytical."

My early difficulty in obtaining writing samples led me to more fully recognize a basic problem in this or any other study of writing. All writing is necessarily grounded in language. Unfortunately, even though we may all be speakers and writers of English, our comprehension and understanding of any piece of writing in English is in some way filtered. My sense is that the TF opposition of the MBTI serves as just such a filter of written discourse.

I am, of course, not the first to suggest such a filter. In the first paragraph of Chapter Six of *Gifts Differing*, Myers and Myers write:

> Thinking and feeling are rival instruments of decision. Both are reasonable and internally consistent, but each works by its own standards. Jolande Jacobi (1968) says that thinking evaluates from the viewpoint "true—false" and feeling from the viewpoint "agreeable—disagreeable." This sounds like a thinker's formulation. "Agreeable" is too pale a word for the rich personal worth of a feeling evaluation. (65)

As any reader might surmise, both Isabel Briggs Myers and Peter B. Myers are F types.

In contrast to the writing of Myers and Myers, we can look at the following passage from *Personality and the Teaching of Composition*, by George H. Jensen and John K. DiTiberio:

> Since thinking types base decisions on logical, objective, and impersonal criteria, and feeling types base theirs on personal, subjective values, the writing of each often reflects respectively an analytical or a personal approach to both content and audience. To use Kinneavy's terms, the writing of thinking types is "thing-centered" and the writing of feeling types is "people-centered" (1971, p.88). The difference further explains yet more qualities of Moffett's I—It and I—You continua. (92)

Jensen and DiTiberio make several points which are important to this discussion. First, they clearly assert that there exist two different discourses. A "thing-centered" discourse is likely to be employed by thinking types. A "people-centered" discourse is likely to be used by feeling types. In addition, if we look at the first two sentences of the Jensen and DiTiberio passage we can see that they are "thing-centered" as opposed to the "people-centered" passage cited from Myers and Myers. When questioned on the authorship of those sentences, Jensen, a T, said that he was the one who initially drafted them. DiTiberio, an F, added only the adverb, "respectively" in revision (personal interview).

With this in mind, we can now move to some of the responses of the initial study. As we compare the T and F responses, we will see that the

T's responded to the prompts objectively and analytically (using Thing-Centered Discourse), regardless of the instructions of the task. On the other hand, F types always responded in a personal (People-Centered Discourse) fashion, despite instructions to do otherwise half the time. Students were asked to respond in writing both "personally" and "analytically" to the following prompt:

Prompt #1 Describe your favorite meal, including the setting (home, restaurant, picnic), the season (why are some foods "winter" and some "summer"?), the total ambiance.

The two students, an ENTJ and an ENFP, responded in the following manner:

Prompt #1	T Student (ENTJ)	F Student (ENFP)
Personal	My favorite meal has two pieces of bread. Between the bread is lettuce, tomato, pickles, and beef. The setting is at a restaurant and can be any time of the year.	My favorite meal is in the Villa. It is in the fall with a dark setting slightly lit by candlelight. The meal starts out with a salad and garlic bread. The main course is Veal Parmesan. I never eat desert, because by this time I am stuffed.
Analytical	My favorite meal has two pieces of bread. Between the bread is lettuce, tomato, pickles, and beef. I like this meal because it is made very fast. The setting is a restaurant. I like the restaurant because it is comfortable.	I chose this meal because I like the romantic setting of the Villa. It is cozy, yet comfortable. I also crave Italian food, because it is something I don't get to eat all the time.

The most obvious point to be made about the ENTJ sample of student writing is that even though the student was supposed to write from two apparently opposing perspectives, he writes almost the identical response both times. There appears to be nothing we can identify as "personal" in the first response. Interestingly enough, we might say that he does do some personalizing in the analytical response, though in a most limited fashion.

The ENFP response differs significantly from the responses given by the ENTJ. Once more there is confusion between the "personal" and the "analytical." Clearly, the response marked "analytical" is personal in nature and is "people-centered." While the response marked "personal" does mention "things," it only does so in order to come to the "people-centered" conclusion of being "stuffed."

Before looking at responses to other prompts, I want to note one other interesting discovery found in the study. While not holding for one hundred percent of the sample, in most instances the actual length of the responses seemed to vary according to type. F types, for the most part, wrote longer "personal" than "analytical" responses. On the other hand, T types generally wrote longer "analytical" than "personal" responses.

Students gave the following writing samples in response to the next writing prompt cited:

Prompt #2 Writing can be an act of ego; unfortunately other people often handle our egos roughly. Have you had an unpleasant experience writing? Was writing ever used as a form of punishment for you in school? Did a teacher overdo the red marks on your writing? Has a colleague rejected your written ideas?

Dredge up a bad experience with writing and record it here. Try to think of a specific experience instead of simply generalizing about bad feelings.

In response to this prompt, I received these interesting responses from an ISTP and an ESFP:

Prompt #2	T Student (ISTP)	F Student (ESFP)
Personal	Yes, writing about subjects or stories that I had no knowledge of; yes, writing papers for punishment; no, I have not had a teacher really overdo the marks on my papers; I have had friends	I've never had a real unpleasant writing experience because I write as little as possible and only when I have to. I did, however, have to write as punishment in the seventh grade. I got in

T Student (ISTP) (*cont.*)	**F Student (ESFP)** (*cont.*)
tell me how to revise and restate ideas but not reject them.	trouble with a few others and we had to write all the a, b, and c's definitions out of my science book. I also once wrote a thesis paper in the tenth grade that I thought was great and I got it back with a low grade and a lot of criticism. I have never had a friend reject my writings because I usually don't let my friends read my writings.

Analytical	Yes, people have had to write about subjects they are not familiar with; yes, people have written papers and even copied pages for punishment; yes, friends have had their papers almost full of marks after doing a paper at the last minute; yes, some people have had their ideas rejected as suggestions from me.	Yes, everyone has had unpleasant writing experiences. My sister had had to write as punishment many times for talking in class. She also once had a teacher who really didn't like her on a report that was due and when she got it back, the teacher had given her a bad grade because she had copied it.

Even though the ISTP student is ostensibly writing about people, including himself, there is a distance in his writing. Indeed, the people he is writing about, himself included, are treated more like "things" than flesh-and-blood humans. Though he is writing about people, his discourse is still "thing-centered." Interestingly, he also makes an allusion to causation in his analysis (a T attribute according to Myers and McCaulley) in which he implies that some papers are marked in red because they were done hastily. It is also interesting that while no one rejects his ideas, he does reject some of the ideas of others.

In contrast, we see language in the ESFP response which is clearly "people-centered." Indeed, the only difference between the response labeled "personal" and the one labeled "analytical" is that the first one concerns itself with the writer herself and the second with another person. For this writer, to be "analytical" apparently means to deal with the world apart from herself; however, that world is not one of things but rather of other people.

These responses were representative of what I received from student writers during the first stage of my research. After consideration and input from colleagues, I determined that while it appeared that the student responses were what I might have expected, it might be interesting to ask students to write from a more "objective" prompt. One of my colleagues suggested, and I think there may be something to it, that the prompts I was using were F prompts which would work at soliciting F responses while troubling Ts. Indeed, the prompts had been written by an F.

In an attempt to overcome this problem during the second round of collecting writing samples, I added a different kind of prompt. In this case I had the students view a small wooden statue of an abstracted human form. Once again, I asked the students to respond both from a "personal" and from an "analytical" point of view.

An INTJ and an ESFP responded to the wooden figure with the following pieces of writing:

	T Student (INTJ)	**F Student (ESFP)**
Analytical	Perhaps this means that we make fun of the crazy too much or that we are wrapped up in our own little world too much to the extent that we are strapped in. Well, I couldn't think of anything else.	This kind of art does not appeal to me at all. I think everyone has one of these type of things at home, but few people are bold enough to show them in public. Very tacky!
Personal	The wooden carving looks comical to me because of the big nose and the way he leans to the right. It looks like he only has one arm that wraps around his body like a straight jacket.	The wooden man reminds me of this gaudy, black thing my grandmother brought me from the Bahamas. The man looks happy.

Again, in the INTJ response we see confusion between "personal" and "analytical." The writing marked "personal" is not "people-centered" at all but rather is interpretive in nature. This is in marked contrast to the response by the ESFP. This F type student is clearly capable of making judgments about the piece of art, but those judgments are of a different nature than the interpretation suggested by the INTJ. Once again, the F type uses people, herself or others, as her focus.

Conclusion and Classroom Implications

The writing samples I have collected, along with the work of other type theory researchers, suggest two distinct types of discourse: a "thing-centered" discourse used by T types and a "people-centered" discourse used by F types. Though these two discourses are different, we do not necessarily have to view them as being mutually exclusive. Indeed, the following diagram may best show how they interact:

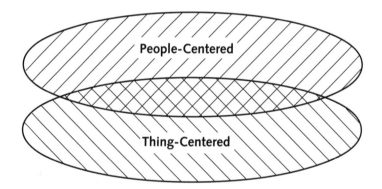

While further research remains to be done in the area of writing development and how it is affected by personality type, it appears that the TF opposition acts as a kind of filter on the writer. I would further suggest that the model of writing development currently in vogue by composition specialists is only partially accurate. F writers are likely to follow the developmental pattern presently accepted. T writers, on the other hand, are more likely to follow the reverse pattern of development. As writers develop, we can expect that they acquire the capability to move into the overlapping area of the two modes of discourse.

Thing-Centered Discourse	People-Centered Discourse
Focus on things—physical world	Focus on humans—emotional
People may be portrayed as objects	Emphasis may be on moods
Tendency to analyze	Tendency to humanize

While all of this is interesting enough, how does it affect classroom teachers whose primary concern is to get their students to develop as writers? I expect the answer to that works in several ways. Teachers need to realize that not all of their students will develop as writers in the same fashion. They should expect their students to grow as writers in different ways. That means that teachers can expect to see some of their students prefer to write "thing-centered discourse" while others will naturally choose "people-centered discourse." Teachers should stress neither discourse over the other. Rather the students' individual writing should be encouraged to develop according to each student's preference. Clearly, while teachers may prefer "people-centered discourse" to "thing-centered discourse," or the other way around, the teachers must understand that their students will be more likely to succeed by beginning to write in accordance with their own preferences, not the preferences of their teachers. Finally, teachers must realize that as they create writing assignments, they will help their students most by assigning a wide range of topics and prompts. By doing so, teachers will allow their students to respond in both their preferred and non-preferred discourse, though it is the teachers' responsibility to guide their students through a combination of both comfortable and uncomfortable territory.

Experiential and descriptive (non-technical) prompts seem to belong more to the world of people-centered discourse. Technical descriptions and assignments which call for real analysis are more likely to belong to the world of thing-centered discourse. Using a combination of assignments calling for both people-centered and thing-centered discourses should give all students an equal chance for success and challenge

Notes

1. Throughout this study I puzzle over which pair of terms (expressive/transactional, personal/analytical, or people-centered/thing-centered) seem to best describe a fundamental difference which parallels the difference between thinking judgment and feeling judgment. Whatever pair of terms we finally decide to use ultimately becomes less important than the hypothesis which begins to emerge here: thinking types and feeling types tend to follow different patterns of development as writers.

Works Cited

Britton, James, Tony Burgess, Nancy Martin, Alex, McLeod, and Harold Rosen. *The Development of Writing Abilities (11–18)*. London: Macmillan Education, 1975.

Elbow, Peter. *Writing Without Teachers*. New York: Oxford University Press, 1973.

———. *Writing with Power*. New York: Oxford University Press, 1985.

Emig, Janet. *The Composing Processes of Twelfth Graders*. Urbana, IL: National Council of Teachers of English, 1971.

Jensen, George H. Personal interview. April 30, 1989.

———. "The Reification of the Basic Writer." *Journal of Basic Writing*. 5 (1986): 52–64.

Jensen, George H. and John K. DiTiberio. "Personality and the Individual Writing Process." *College Composition and Communication*. 35 (1984): 285–300.

———. *Personality and the Teaching of Composition*. Norwood, NJ: Ablex, 1989.

Kinneavy, James. *A Theory of Discourse*. Englewood Cliffs, NJ: Prentice-Hall, 1971.

Moffet, James. *Teaching the Universe of Discourse*. Boston: Houghton Mifflin, 1968.

Myers, Isabel Briggs with Peter B. Myers. *Gifts Differing*. Palo Alto, CA: Consulting Psychologists Press, 1980.

Myers, Isabel Briggs and Mary H. McCaulley. *Manual: A Guide to the Development and Use of the Myers-Briggs Type Indicator*. Palo Alto, CA: Consulting Psychololgists Press, 1985.

4   Comfortable Clothes:
Using Type to Design Assignments

Maurice Scharton and Janice Neuleib

It would be quite possible to write a lot of pat persuasive rubbish about type and assignments. The tidiness of type theory invites glib generalizations about honoring differences and personalizing instruction. And teachers, as Hillocks observes in his discussion of assignments in *Research in Written Composition*, often nourish a fantasy that assignments hold some special power to unlock writing competence. So it is wise to begin this discussion by acknowledging two disconcerting facts: 1) that writing behavior, which is learned, often runs counter to what would seem true to type, and 2) that assignments must conform to institutional, programmatic goals before they take account of individual preferences. Readers are cautioned to screen the ensuing text through those facts. Within those constraining facts, we can offer some "clinical" observations based on teaching experience conditioned by our knowledge of personality type theory and writing research. We can also offer sensible advice about how to use typological language and ideas to create writing assignments that encourage people to reflect on writing processes. And we can advance a few thoughts about directions that type theory and assignment practice may take together.

For us, this essay is situated on a narrow but rather deep confluence of two areas of competence. Our knowledge of type theory and application comes mainly in the context of tutoring situations (see "The Gift of Insight"). Since personality plays a major role in tutorial interactions, per-

47

sonality type offers both insight and language useful to tutors. Our knowledge of assignments grows in large part from the context of writing assessment (see "Models of Competence"), which relies on refined and technically sophisticated assignments to produce valid and reliable assessment. Those two areas of competence came together in type-based writing assignments in a textbook we recently wrote (*Inside/Out: A Guide to Writing*). The main criteria of our assignment-making process for that textbook were that assignments ought to feel "natural"; that is, they ought to proceed from the nature of the writer in the situation; and that in a process of learning to write, assignments should give reflection on writing priority over production of text. Acceptable texts are in a very real sense only by-products of learning to write.

Functions of Writing Assignments

Before moving into our type-based clinical observations, advice, and propositions, we would like to build a framework of composition theory and research. To begin with, it is useful to consider what academic forces shape assignments and how those assignments in turn shape writer's experiences of writing. Debates over assignments in school writing date back at least to Emig's original work on twelfth graders in which she noted that students write more eagerly and successfully when they write for their own purposes such as notes, stories, or diaries and that they write less successfully, or less willingly, when the assignments are school-sponsored (*The Composing Processes of Twelfth Graders*). The expressivist movement, embodied in Peter Elbow's *Writing Without Teachers*, suggested that writers write best when they write for their own purposes. Of course, the definition of good writing in these studies begs the question since the researchers begin with the assumption that good writing occurs when the writer is engaged with and involved in the writing task. These early expressivist theorists objected to group assignments because they supposedly thwarted creativity. Such may be true, but not all writing situations foreground creativity.

In fact, group assignments do have a place in the rigid uniformity of national and regional writing assessments. In fact, the wider and more comprehensive an assessment, the more uniform the assignment must be. Such uniformity can lead to rigidity in some situations. At least in the state of Illinois where we teach, the bureaucrats who run the state writing assessment reward and privilege five-paragraph essays and school-sponsored writing. Thus "creativity" is sacrificed to the limits necessary so that standardized assignments will gain regularized results.

Assignments in assessment must be uniform in as many ways as possible. We have read essays for the Educational Testing Advanced Placement English Language and Literature tests for several years and have continuously noted the energy that goes into developing uniformity and consistency in these tests. For a test like the Advanced Placement Language exam, test developers must first create assignments that ask for essays that will resemble the assignments given in courses likely to be replaced by test results. These assignments are then field tested in college classrooms, reviewed for effectiveness in measuring the writers' performance, and then finally used in the national test. Thus from one year to the next, AP questions have predictable similarities, subject to change only when the nature of college writing courses themselves change.

As is often the case, the questions themselves tend to cause debate about the supposed and proposed nature of a college writing course. The 1994 Advanced Placement English Language questions included cuttings of essays from the era of Charles II of England and from a collection of essays by Joan Didion. The assignments caused high school teachers to ask whether these essays were indeed emblematic of readings from freshman composition courses and what responses a college writing teacher would expect from the average student, meaning the student who has preferences other than NP. Assessments with such questions can easily begin to drive assignment giving in writing courses at both the advanced high school level and the college level, unless the conversations among test developers and writing teachers and researchers continue to be open and productive. In his first book on testing, Edward White stresses the need for both rigid control of testing situations and open discussions among teachers and testers (*Teaching and Assessing Writing*).

Testing researchers debate the optimal nature of these prescribed assignments for assessment (Brossell). Issues of performance versus communication become a part of the debate, especially the debate about the effectiveness of rhetorical versus scenario assignments. Rhetorical assignments ask the writer to consider the potential audience in developing an argumentative or informative essay. For example, a prompt we used in a regional assessment workshop asked student writers to persuade the school administration that junk food should be forbidden in the school cafeteria. (This topic evoked some fascinating essays, especially from third and sixth graders.)

A scenario assignment develops a problem in context, often the kind of moral dilemma associated with the Perry, Kohlberg, or Gilligan scales. For example, a student knows that a good friend is using a crib sheet with written answers to a test, that the teacher will exact severe punishment, and that others in the class also know of the circumstance. The writer has to discuss the moral dilemma of the student who knows of the crib sheet and of the possible disapproval of both teacher and peers. These kinds of questions are often used in research into social and intellectual development of writers (Huizinga).

Elements of the Assignment

Modes and Topics

Perhaps the most conventional means of building assignments, both in current traditional rhetoric and in classical rhetoric, centered on various categories of writing. The modes (or *topoi* in Aristotle: definition, comparison, cause and effect, etc.; see Corbett) vary in categorization from text to text, but generally modes describe naturally occurring patterns of thought. Current writing research, as we noted earlier, argues that no one sets out to write in a mode (unless, of course, a teacher assigns it). In fact, modes are, if we can believe Kant, the way that the human mind works, so they happen automatically when we begin to write or talk about any subject. If we believe the postmodern theorists, then no set categories occur, and modes are an absurd choice. Either way, it does not make much sense to ask writers to conform to an artificial pattern exclusive of their inclinations. We are not suggesting that assignments be planned around our observations of writers using the modes, but writers should find their own comfort zones within these kinds of boundaries. Both of us, for example, who are intuitives, are quite happy composing in the most restrictive of writing forms, such as sonnets and sestinas, grant proposals and curriculum vitae.

Turning to some specific observations apropos of type and assignment, we would suggest that to set out to write in a mode can be distracting for many. We have found in our work with personality type that mode-related assignments work against the types most inclined to use them. Sensing types tend to become frustrated with the modes because they try to stay within the required forms and are limited by the restrictions. In both classroom and testing situations, intuitive types tend to find the modes enjoyable in the same ways that they enjoy creative assignments. Modes challenge their imaginations to work around the requirements of the form and be creative anyway. The modes resemble the sonnet form in some ways. They limit too severely the writer who is already constrained by convention. They enable and entertain writers who tend to break the boundaries anyway.

Audience

Form alone certainly cannot account for most of the assignments given in English classes (or even non-English classes). Rhetorical considerations often dominate assignment choices. Speech rhetoric deals specifically with the demographics of real audiences. Many assignments, especially for high school writers, ask for the writer to consider demographics of real readers or to write for live readers. Thus an assignment for such writers would ask about the nature of the audience who would attend a speech on a political or social issue. How old are they? Where do they live? What political leanings do they have? The speech writer then slants the speech to fit these attitudes and experiences of the audience. Extraverts are often comfortable with near audiences since the world of the writer is most immediate in this contextualized situation.

We use an assignment in *Inside/Out* that is rather an old chestnut: write a letter describing an adventure at camp to a parent, a friend, and a romantic partner. This assignment provides a quick and easy view of the different content that will be included in texts written for specific audiences, especially for those readers the writer knows best. Once again, this type of immediate writing activity appeals to writers with extraverted preferences since it involves person-to-person communication about an extraverted activity (i.e., an adventure).

Quite the opposite circumstances dominate when the audience is abstract and distant. Too often school-sponsored writing fits this description. The writing circumstance is not transactional (Britton) but rather clearly for purposes of evaluation. Thus when a writer is asked to respond to a prompt in a regional or national assessment, the audience is the abstract general audience of the academic essay, but with none of the immediacy of conversation intrinsic in professional journal publication. Thus the writer must deal with an abstract audience that is in many ways a composite of all the teachers and raters who have ever read essays written for school and assessment.

Much of our teaching experience has occurred with intuitive feeling types, who predominate in virtually every class that satisfies English major or minor requirements. We also have considerable experience (as well as personal knowledge) of the processes and problems of intuitive thinking types, amongst whom we are numbered. The writers who are most comfortable with the abstract audience are those who have already integrated the system and conventions of academic writing into their writing repertoires. These writers understand almost instinctively what the academy demands and how those demands work out in practice. The types who probably are most comfortable with the abstract audience of the academic essay are those who will naturally find their ways into the academy, the introverted intuitive types. Perhaps, in fact, academic writing for an abstract audience is the natural mode of introverted intuitive types, since the type tables indicate that most academics fall into these categories (cf., Macdaid, McCaulley, and Kainz).

Forum

We find it perplexing that the word which most accurately describes a public speech has come to mean exactly the opposite in academic parlance. Thus, a forum now means the place of publication or printed appearance, not the place of presentation.

Self-sponsored writing like personal letters and writers' journals are often the valued property of the types most likely to be writers (cf., Macdaid, et al. 99, 106, and 108). Intuitive feeling types write more letters and both keep and encourage the keeping of journals by others. We have been maintaining records of the type preferences of future high school English teachers for six years. Our records confirm the type tables in that most of these future teachers are intuitive feeling types. Our experience with these future teachers confirms that they write more letters than any other type and that they both keep self-sponsored journals and want to give journal assignments to their classes. The lines from *The Importance of Being Earnest* come to mind that a young girl's diary is a record of her deepest personal experiences and thus meant for publication. The journal often becomes a repository for writers' ideas for future writing, as a colleague of ours found in her work with the manuscripts and notes of scores of professional writers. Their personal journals were the beginning points for much of their future work (Fennick). Again, the type tables indicate that professional writers tend to be intuitive feeling types (Macdaid, et al. 97).

The popular forums include writing for every kind of media, including radio and television, though we usually categorize the popular magazines among the common reading of most student writers in our classes. We ask them to categorize their reading in order to give them a sense of the appropriate forum for the writing they are likely to do in response to those forums they most often read. Again, this "assignment" runs according to type. Writers tend to read the materials that suit their temperaments. Intuitive feeling types are more likely to read *The New Yorker* than sensing thinking types, and certainly more likely to write for *The New Yorker*. We find that sensing perceiving types are more likely to read sports magazines and much more likely to write for this kind of forum if given their preferences. Often intuitive thinking types read cyberpunk science fiction magazines, and arguably only they would write for them. We have a cyberpunk science fiction course offered occasionally in our department, and the clientele includes almost all introverted intuitive thinking types. We don't usually have sensing feeling types in our classes—most English majors are intuitives—but the sample we have from Writing Project teachers suggests that SFs enjoy women's magazines about cooking and decorating or about parenting and crafts.

The intellectual forums are fairly obvious for the readers of this essay. They are what college professors read and publish within, though we often have some misgivings about exposing the young to these forums before they have been carefully warned that these journals have more in common with performative school-sponsored writing than they do with magazines that people really want to either write for or read from. We will hope that that last sentence is buried and hidden from our faculty evaluative committees, but we feel like C. S. Lewis who said that perhaps because he lived in the provinces he had never known anyone who read the Bible as literature. Perhaps it is because we live in the midwest, but we have never known anyone who read either school-sponsored writing or professional journals for pleasure. The types who write for them are of course in the four corners of the type table (TJ) and the introverted intuitive quadrant, college professors and professionals of various sorts.

Purpose

James Britton categorized writing as either transactional or expressive (i.e., nontransactional) in purpose. James Kinneavy characterized writing as having one of four purposes: to persuade, to inform, to express, or to be artistic. All four can be transactional, but clearly conveying information is the most transactional of aims since readers are most interested in getting the news of the day from transactional forums like newspapers and CNN. In a school setting, however, any of these forms can be merely performative if the goal is simply to get a grade. Certainly, much school-sponsored writing pretends to be informational, for example the content on a test, but it is really performative since the intended reader (i.e., the instructor) already knows the information. The purpose for the writer in such contexts may be to convey information, but the reader intends only to evaluate—not much fun for either, really.

Truly transactional assignments should be aimed at the writer who has a purpose in conveying information as in news reporting and the like. Persuasion seldom pleases anyone, and probably should be reserved for thinking types who are performing before a debate judge or in a court of law. Otherwise, persuasion tends to be difficult and unpleasant for both writers and readers. At times, writers of college essay anthologies mistake expressive writing for argumentation or persuasion and confuse writers considerably by the labeling of categories. Essays such as those generally found on subjects like race and abortion intend to declare the stand of the writers and usually have little intention of affecting the actions of the readers. Assigning such essays and pretending that they are argumentative or persuasive merely confuses nearly everyone in class, most especially the teaching assistant who cannot figure out why the class cannot write argument. We apologize for this aside, but we should note that we have taught graduate teaching assistants for many years and debated this issue at length.

Type Theory and Composing Practice

Still, some writers prefer professional writing to personal, and others the reverse. Jensen and DiTiberio's *Personality and the Teaching of Composi-*

tion discusses who likes which kind of writing and who prefers which kinds of assignments. Exercises using descriptions of time (18–28) characterize worldviews that then drive individual writing interests. The authors theorize that feeling types must care about their subjects and that thinking types must categorize the topic in various satisfactory ways. These distinctions seem particularly important for assignment giving, since the person composing the assignments much take both these needs into account. Even though we began by saying that we resist traditional assignments, even when we direct writers toward their own interests, we are careful to keep this theoretical warning in mind. Feeling types must have a commitment to their writing projects, and thinking types must have a logical understanding of where the project fits into their mental maps.

In our own research and teaching, we have tried to keep these preferences in mind as we give assignments. We and our graduate students have worked extensively with the writing type preference exercises in *Inside/Out* and have found that several generalizations can be added to those made by Jensen and DiTiberio. Extraverts want to move through assignment acquisition and planning as quickly as possible. In workshops with extraverts and introverts in separate groups, we have found that the extraverts create an entire writing assignment through to distribution of the finished product to appropriate audiences. They tend to be this thorough even when asked only to discuss the disposition of an assignment. Introverts tend, on the other hand, to spend time on the planning stages and, if working in a group, to spend considerable time negotiating project activities and directions.

Writers with a sensing preference tend to accept the boundaries of an assignment, but want the freedom to pursue their own designs within those boundaries. Writers with intuitive preferences tend to want limits that can direct their creativity and, incidentally, their tendencies to run too free with their associations. Intuitive thinking type writers especially find it helpful to have a challenging rhetorical situation that will trigger the first rush of creativity, a conference call for papers, for example, or a teacher who gives the impossible assignment, anything for a challenge. Intuitive feeling type writers find challenge less interesting in assignments than an intriguing possibility that will give them a chance to explore and discover new areas of the psyche or the world of fiction and fantasy.

In judging and perceiving we have found few surprises, except that each can learn much from the other about work patterns. In group work, perceiving types can learn to use the energy of judging types to get early planning on an assignment out of the way, and judging types can learn to wait for that final spurt of energy in the perceiving types to discover some late hour new insight about the possible redirection of a project. This help interaction works as long as no one kills anyone else.

Clinical Experience with Type in Writing Classes

In the introductory chapters of *Inside/Out*, we ask writers to investigate their writing preferences as reflected in the MBTI format (19–20). One of the activities, aimed at distinguishing sensing and intuitive preferences, asks participants to discuss their favorite kinds of writing assignments. We have found that writers with a clear sensing preference want "freedom" in their assignments. They have told us that freedom to them means that they do not want an assignment that forces them into the current academic mold of heavy theorizing. Writers with an intuitive preference, however, describe assignments that trigger the imagination, the more theoretical or the zanier the better. Thus a favorite teacher for the writer with a sensing preference will be the one who allows the writer to use standard research techniques and to write within clearly defined (by the writer) guidelines. For the writer with an intuitive preference, a teacher who provides inventive and exciting possibilities will more likely get both student approval and inventive student papers.

The obvious point, of course, is that the teacher with a sensing preference will prefer to give writing activities that encourage the kinds of "freedom" described by the sensing writers using the MBTI activity. One instructor with a strong sensing preference told us that she gives an assignment that asks writers to investigate the meanings of their names. This assignment gives direction and provides a clear research goal without requiring the writers to draw complex conclusions or to make discoveries "out of nothing." On the other hand, a student with a strong intuitive preference described her favorite assignment as coming from a teacher in a Renaissance and Reformation class who asked each member of the class to write about the character in that historical period who thought or acted most like the writer. In this instance the student writers had to make intuitive leaps about the combined factors such as the nature of the historical era, the historical figures in the context of the class materials, and the relationship of all these factors to themselves as current historical figures. The teacher clearly wanted this kind of stretching and would have been displeased with a concise report on a fifteenth or sixteen century historical figure, no matter the quality of the research.

Since high school teachers are statistically more likely to be sensing types (at least in disciplines other than English), the likelihood of the reporting type of assignment coming from a high school may be greater, whereas the creative assignment that asks the writer to invent and imagine, even in history class, would more likely emerge from a college professor who would statistically be more likely to be intuitive (Macdaid, et al. 243, 255).

At this point, we would like to advance some thoughts about typological approaches to assignments. We caution the reader to keep in mind that there is no one so certain and self-assured in argument as an intuitive who has little or no empirical information to interfere with his or her theoretical speculations.

As we have indicated, our experiences tell us that a simple interpretation of type descriptions can cause confusion for the teacher or editor who expects certain behaviors from sensing and intuitive types. Sensing type writers are not necessarily linear in their writing styles. Rather they tend to find assignments important that allow them to work within a prescribed structure in their own ways. We think that this need to have individual freedom in writing may explain the long history of clinging to the modes as assignment forms. The modes do not drive a writer's topic, only the form. The writer is still free to develop a topic that fits like comfortable clothes. Intuitives like the modes for different reasons, mostly because they are a chance to kick against the traces a bit and find out where the limits will take the imagination. Better than modes for an intuitive, however, are the equivalent of a conference theme or call for papers. A topic similar to a national conference call like "New Directions for Fork-Lift Design" or "Planning a Retirement in Alaska" can amuse and intrigue an intuitive. Can the writing project be done with these limitations, and even better with the writer's lack of knowledge in the field? Many intuitives rise to such bait; some even give themselves such topics if an accommodating teacher or conference chair does not oblige with some such limit.

Dr. Irene Brosnahan has been working with us for several years on the relationship between learning grammar and personality preference. One of the most intriguing results of the studies has been the discovery that intuitive feeling types, and to a lesser extent sensing feeling types, learn grammar only when they find a reason to like the subject. They also certainly cannot write papers about language learning and teaching without becoming interested and engaged in the topic. Thinking types, on the contrary, either learn it or do not, write about it or do not, without much reference to the affective response to the subject.

In our observations of these future teachers of language and writing, we have found consistently that, since they tend to be intuitive feeling types for the most part, it is wise to give assignments that tempt their enthusiasms and values. If not, they will tend to ossify their opinions and latch on to current conventional wisdom that learning grammar helps no one to write better. They never bother to learn what grammar is for unless they find out first that they like it. This issue is extremely important since by far the large majority of future and current English teachers are intuitive feeling types (Brosnahan and Neuleib).

Judging and perceiving preferences can affect the timing for completing assignments. We have discovered the strength of this connection in MBTI workshops when we ask participants when they begin work on a long (ten pages or more) paper. When we ask who has started by, say, the night before the paper is due, all hands are raised, but as we move farther from the due date, the hands go down in nearly exact correlation with the judging and perceiving preferences. The stronger the judging preference, the earlier the paper begins, and vice versa. Assignments for long projects probably should be given as early as possible but repeated over a three or four week period to catch each of the levels of judging and perceiving preference. In addition, work groups probably should have a mix of perceiving and judging types so that the groups can have equal advantage from the differing strengths contributed by these preferences (to repeat our caveat, as long as everyone stays alive).

Finally, our practical observations have provided a seeming contradiction. We have noted that INTPs, though introverts, do not like assignments that ask for personal introspection. They tend to turn self-discovery into a research project rather than a self-discovery process. Many of our INTP friends and students find assignments for themselves that have to do with the discovery of the processes of the mind, a mind from which no feelings flow, thank you. They are, therefore, the ultimate research machines when it comes to assignments. They will turn any assignment into a research project—and as teachers, they add research to any assignment sequence. Neuleib, an INTJ, insisted on a freshman English assignment for which every writer must do original field research (INTJs do not think that going to the library and looking up books and magazines is research) for all incoming freshmen at ISU.

When it comes to what to do with assignments, we have been surprised by the preferences of ISTJ students. Introverted judging types need to rest and invite their souls. The ultimate sensing judging types, they might seem to be the most steady and sturdy in their interests. We have found, however, that ISTJ writers often show a whimsy in their assignment choices that stresses the sensing preference. They want masses of information that they can sort and enjoy in a variety of ways. Thus they need assignments that pull them away from routine activities and lead them into the world of detail and multiple interests. One of our colleagues, a strong ISTJ, enjoys reading and writing about gardening as well as indulging in the hobby. She likes masses of information and multiple possibilities, and she wants her freedom to design her projects to suit herself. We have indicated our surprise at the tendencies of sensing judging types to want freedom of construction in their writing activities. They want writing assignments that allow them to find as much information as possible and enjoy the luxury of working with it in their own ways for their own purposes. They want assignments that enable that particular kind of freedom.

Sensing perceiving types also like information, but they tend to want less contemplation of the material and more production of text. They are the exciting and breathless writers who may surprise a teacher by producing an original and startling piece for even a relatively standard assignment, but they will do it at the last minute, and they will not revise. That job is for the editor, while the sensing perceiving type is free to wander on to another topic. We surmise that Hemingway was probably a sensing perceiving type, and his editor, Maxwell Perkins, would probably have agreed as he reworked Hemingway's text while the great man headed off on his next sporting adventure.

Intuitive thinking types like freedom too—and elegance, but they want to argue while being free and elegant. Earlier we spoke against persuasive and argumentative writing. For intuitive thinking types, we will suggest just the opposite. Not that anyone wants to listen to them argue or read their arguments, but they do so enjoy arguing with one another and with themselves that it seems a kindness to give them agonistic assignments. Collections of law briefs are nice for this purpose, and do no harm to the rest of the class.

When we say that intuitive thinking types like elegance, we mean that they like for assignments to be subtle, simple, and wondrously challenging. The more difficult, the better. The more boring, the better, for the intuitive thinking will love the challenge of finding something to do with the project. We usually tell teachers to leave intuitive thinking type students alone. Give them a mere crust of an assignment, send them off to the library, and keep them away from the rest of the students. Well, it is what our teachers did with us.

Intuitive feeling types want a different type of freedom. As we indicated earlier, by far the majority of creative writers are intuitive feeling types. These writers need few assignments that come from the outside; in fact, they often keep journals and notebooks with writing ideas at hand. They make their own assignments if someone does not offer one. They might need an early journal requirement so that they can find their own best ways of writing, but chances are good that the journal or writing log will stay with the writer far beyond the limits of the class in which it is begun.

As we have indicated from our grammar research, we have observed that English majors, especially future teachers, tend to be intuitive feeling types. This preference affects assignment giving in English classes and even affects the debates over the nature of writing. Intuitive feeling types tend to see writing as a deeply involving personal process that has intense interest and individual importance for each writer. Thus these English teachers will lean toward such movements as the expressivist movement of the sixties and the process movement of the eighties. They will resist set forms, critique formalist rhetoric, and encourage personal involvement in writing assignments. This approach works well as long as these teachers keep in mind that the rest of the school or university may have much different values and expectations.

Conclusion: Sweatclothes and Straitjackets

Since you cannot anticipate what people will like and cannot even count on them to give you an accurate reading of their type, and since writing processes are learned behavior, it makes the most sense to simply provide some alternate structures and to allow people to choose the one that feels the most comfortable. We began this essay with this principle and finish with it. The exceptions are many, of course. Everyone must learn to write to assessment questions that are uniform, even though some types may be more comfortable with the challenge to creativity in the uniformity. Since intuitive types have fun with prescribed assignments (e.g., sestinas and conference calls for papers), teachers who allow students to choose assignments should also spend time thinking up challenging topics that will allow creative imaginations to soar. We suggest that teachers, however, help young writers learn to flap their wings in the safe environment of their own interests before they soar to the heights of controlled assessment questions in the rarified air of AP, SAT, GMAT, or doctoral essays.

Works Cited

Brosnahan, Irene, and Janice Neuleib. "Teaching Grammar Affectively: Learning to Like Grammar." *The Place of Grammar in Writing Instruction: Past, Present, Future*. Ray Wallace and Susan Hunter, eds. Portsmouth, NH: Heinemann, 1995.

Britton, James, et al. *The Development of Writing Abilities*. London: Macmillan, 1975.

Brossell, Gordon. "Rhetorical Specification in Essay Examination Topics." *College English* 45 (1983): 165–173.

Corbett, Edward P.J. *Classical Rhetoric for the Modern Student*. New York: Oxford UP, 1990.

Elbow, Peter. *Writing Without Teachers*. New York: Oxford UP, 1973.

Emig, Janet. *The Composing Processes of Twelfth Graders*. Urbana, IL: NCTE, 1971.

Faigley, Lester. *Fragments of Reality: Postmodernity and the Subject of Composition*. Pittsburgh: U of Pittsburgh P, 1992.

Fennick, Ruth. "The Creative Processes of Prose-Fiction Writers: What They Suggest for Teaching Composition." Diss. Illinois State, 1991.

Gilligan, Carol. *In a Different Voice: Psychological Theory and Women's Development*. Cambridge, MA: Harvard UP, 1982.

Huizinga, Mark. "Moral Development and the Composition Classroom." Master's Thesis, Illinois State, 1993.

Jensen, George H. & DiTiberio, John K. "Personality and Individual Writing Processes." *College Composition and Communication* 35 (1984): 285–289.

——. *Personality and the Teaching of Composition*. Norwood, NJ: Ablex, 1989.

Macdaid, Gerald, Mary McCaulley, and Richard Kainz, eds. *Atlas of Type Tables*. Gainesville, FL: CAPT, 1986.

McCaulley, Mary, and Frank Natter. *Psychological (Myers-Briggs) Type Differences in Education*. Gainesville, FL: CAPT, 1974.

Kohlberg, Lawrence. *The Psychology of Moral Development: Essays on Moral Development*. San Francisco: Harper, 1984.

Moffett, James. *Teaching the Universe of Discourse*. Boston: Houghton Mifflin, 1968.

Perry, Walter. *Forms of Intellectual and Ethical Development in the College Years, A Scheme.* New York: Holt, 1968.

Scharton, Maurice, and Janice Neuleib. "The Gift of Insight: Personality Type, Tutoring, and Learning." *Expanding and Changing the Writing Center: New Directions.* Ray Wallace and Jeanne Simpson, eds. New York: Garland Press, 1990, 184–204.

———. *Inside/Out: A Guide to Writing.* Boston: Allyn & Bacon, 1993.

———. "Models of Competence: Responses to a Scenario Writing Assignment." *Research in the Teaching of English*, 23, 163–180.

White, Edward. *Teaching and Assessing Writing.* San Francisco: Jossey-Bass, 1985.

5   The Role of Personality Preferences in Readable Writing

Alice S. Horning

In the last decade or so, literacy scholars have been focusing more and more intently on the psychological processes in writing and in reading. Recent publications include such titles as Jensen and DiTiberio's *Personality and the Teaching of Composition*, Scribner and Cole's *The Psychology of Literacy*, and my cross-disciplinary exploration, *The Psycholinguistics of Readable Writing*. Our understanding of the psycholinguistic factors in reading and writing has shown marked development from these discussions. Despite these publications, however, one area of inquiry within the psycholinguistics of literacy has not been getting as much attention as it warrants due not only to the inherent complexity of literacy, but also to researchers' general tendency to focus on issues oriented to one perspective only.

This area needing greater attention addresses how readers and writers interact with one another in readable writing. I have defined readable writing in *The Psycholinguistics of Readable Writing* as occurring "when writers have specific intentions that are realized in conventions of text . . . so that readers can set up specific expectations and confirm them . . ." (88). Readable text, produced consciously by writers and processed in particular ways by readers, demands attention; it has theoretical and practical implications for teaching and learning reading, writing and critical literacy. Personality type theory applied to text processing illuminates the nature of the reader-writer interaction in readable writing. Four case studies to be presented here demonstrate the relevance of personality type theory for teaching and learning readable writing and show that peer exchange of texts among students aware of type theory can be more specific and useful than is usually the case.

Some of the most interesting psycholinguistic research in the last few years examines the role of personality in literacy. This research draws largely on the proposals of the Swiss psychologist Carl Jung. As noted in Chapter 1, personality type theory suggests that individuals' psychic energy may be extraverted or introverted, that they gather information through sensing or intuitive perception, they make decisions with thinking or feeling judgment, and they prefer a judging or perceiving life style. The information-gathering and decision-making functions, discussed in Chapter 1 as the dominant functions, are particularly important to the creation of readable texts. The cases to be discussed below show the usefulness of the dominant functions of personality (the information-gathering and decision-making functions) in explaining key features of critical literacy, and provide an analysis of readers' and writers' strategies relevant to their meeting in readable writing.

Type and Literacy

In literacy, two general kinds of activity must go on, and these fit quite precisely into the personality type analysis of dominant function. First, of the four functions basic to the overall organization of personality, two have to do with gathering information about the world: the sensing and intuition functions. Reading is clearly one way to gather information about the world, and one which is currently essential to adaptation in our information-oriented society. When readers must use this information to make decisions, the thinking and feeling functions come into play. Readers and writers must find common ground among these four functions to meet successfully in texts. That is, a readable text produced by a writer and comprehended by a reader will provide a balance of these four functions. Achieving this balance requires work on the part of both participants in a text-based transaction. In peer exchange, writers have an opportunity to talk with readers whose dominant types differ from their own and can get more focused and useful feedback through the use of readers' dominant function-based responses.

On the writers' side, there is a natural preference to present information in ways consistent with a kind of "Do Unto Others" principle. That is, writers who prefer to get sense-based information will provide that kind of information in their texts. The material will be factually based, focused on concrete detail, and often lacking in examples. (As a sensing writer, I have been told repeatedly by readers that I need to give more examples—including in this particular paragraph, which did not even exist in an earlier draft of this paper.) On the intuitive side, writers will tend to write about patterns and abstractions, and leave out the concrete details that are needed. Similarly in the decision-making dimension, feeling types will offer texts that reach out to readers without much concern for logical organization or reasoning. Thinking types present clearly reasoned arguments for their ideas, but do little to connect with readers.

Probably the single most important point proposed by George Jensen and John DiTiberio in their insightful book, *Personality and the Teaching of Composition*, is that writers need to learn to balance their own preferences against those of readers who may be at the opposite end of each dimension (129–131). Moreover, in my experience, when type theory either informs classroom teaching or when it is presented overtly, students have a much easier time using suggested strategies to create more readable writing. Personality type theory's value lies in its support for the presentation of alternative strategies for presenting information as useful alternatives rather than black-white, right-wrong dichotomies. Jensen and DiTiberio make an equally valid point about readers' preferences influencing their judgments, particularly important for teachers in evaluating writing. They point out that just as writers present information in ways consistent with their dominant strategies, so readers too will have preferences for texts consistent with their types. Like writers, readers (i.e., teachers) need to learn to balance their non-preferred and preferred approaches to texts in their evaluations and responses (Jensen and DiTiberio 139–140).

Very little empirical research has been done to test the relevance of personality type for aspects of literacy. One study, reported in 1989, showed that the thinking-feeling dimension of type is pertinent to reading comprehension (Singer). Preference for thinking or feeling influences comprehension according to the results, such that subjects in the study

> with a feeling preference make more accurate decisions on comprehensive multiple choice tests when the text is narrative, while students with a

thinking preference do better on the more logically arranged, formally presented expository texts. (Singer 33)

This study focused on reading to the exclusion of writing. Jensen and DiTiberio's work touches on reader-writer interaction briefly and with particular focus on readers in their chapter on how teachers evaluate writing (133–40), as noted above. In *The Psycholinguistics of Readable Writing*, I have examined the ways in which type influences readers' responses to texts and their recommendations for revision. Besides these studies and the ones in this volume, there has been little work on the ways in which personality preferences influence text processing and the ways in which readers and writers interact on paper.

Frank Smith, though not addressing personality type directly, explores the meeting ground of writers and readers in detail in his chapter on "The Writer-Reader Contract" in *Writing and the Writer*. Smith argues that when readers and writers come together in the "middle ground of the text" (88), readers' expectations must coincide with writers' intentions if they are to meet. Moreover, Smith points out that both the expectations and the intentions are largely, though not entirely, unconscious in nature. How these become explicit according to Smith, at least on the production side, is through the use of conventions in writing. By conventions, Smith means both larger organizational strategies of text such as genre schemes and discourse structures and the more specific strategies of sentence formation. He notes that

> the central point about conventions is that they are what people *expect*, and as I have already argued briefly, language is only understood because readers (and listeners) can form expectations about what is going to be said. (93)

Readers form expectations which writers confirm through their use of conventions. Comprehension of readable text comes about when, as Smith says,

> the writer's intentions and the readers' expectations coincided completely, when every intention of the author was correctly anticipated by the reader, and when every expectation of the reader was fulfilled. (96)

Personality type theory and the concept of dominant functions help account for how such comprehension comes about, or why it doesn't, as the cases below will show.

These expectations and conventions come together in a text in a very specific way that Smith describes as follows:

> The conventions of the text reflect both the intentions that the writer expresses and the meanings that the reader anticipates. It is upon the conventions that the perspectives of writer and reader converge and intersect. The reader relies upon the writer to employ them and the writer relies upon the reader to expect them. Conventions are the contract on which writers and readers must agree if the text is to be comprehended .... (96)

The cases to be discussed below will show that the writers' choice of conventions is tied closely to personality type and particularly to the dominant function, and that readers' responses reflect their dominant types as well. The choices of writers and their impact on readers show up clearly in all cases.

Case Studies of Writers and Readers

As a reminder, type theory suggests that although personality preferences shape our attitudes and the way we function in the world generally, one preference is most prominent in an individual's personality. This is the one described in Chapter 1 as the dominant preference. The dominant is either an information-gathering function (sensing or intuition) or a decision-making function (thinking or feeling). The dominant is the most fully developed preference, and the most trusted function for each individual. The cases to be discussed here show the role of the dominant in how writers present their ideas in text and how readers respond. Understanding the nature of this interaction can help readers, writers and teachers with readable writing through balancing writers' preferences against those of readers. The cases involve writers with each of the possible dominant functions (sensing, intuition, thinking and feeling) and the reactions of readers of the same or different dominant function.

The subjects in these four cases are all students in a research paper course at a medium-sized public university in the midwest. All subjects have provided written permission for the use of their writing, their reported MBTI results and other information. In each case to be discussed here, the writer prepared a full draft of a research paper on a career-related topic or issue, and other students read the paper and responded to it.

The readers' responses were written on a guided worksheet given to all students and discussed in small group sessions, and writers and readers provided their reported MBTI results on the worksheet as well.

The data in these cases may be slanted by several factors. The worksheet itself skews the readers' responses in certain ways as did the influence of aspects of writing discussed in class and in the materials used in the course. The students' responses to one another are inevitably focused on their general perception of the teacher's evaluation criteria, based on all their other work (four completed papers plus revisions prior to this assignment). The discussion of each case will focus largely on the opening paragraph of the paper, on which considerable time had been spent in class. Inevitably, personality preferences have a complex impact on people and preferences play out with a great deal of individual variation, so that a focus on the dominant function may be misleading and oversimplified. And, various difficulties with the use of the MBTI as a psychological instrument should be kept in mind (Pittenger). Despite the influence of these variables, the influence on presentation of each of the four dominant types among the writers and the strong role of the dominant type in readers' reactions will nevertheless be clear.

Figure 1 gives an overview of the cases in terms of each writer's dominant function and the dominant for all of the readers.

Figure 1. Case study writers' and readers' dominant types.

Case	Writer's dominant	Reader's dominant
1	Sensing	S, S, F, N
2	Intuition	S, S, F
3	Thinking	S, T, F
4	Feeling	S, S, S

In each case, the writer has feedback from readers who share the same dominant and/or from readers of a different dominant type. Although it is often difficult to make good use of feedback in peer editing, type theory allows writers not only to get the positive responses of readers whose needs are fully met in the text but also to make use of a deeper understanding of the needs of readers of differing dominant types.

Subject 1: Sensing dominant

Subject 1's type is ISFJ (introverted, sensing, feeling, judging), and although she was not a first-year student when she took the research paper course, she was particularly interested in career exploration. The opening paragraph of her paper reads as follows:

> In the past, whenever someone asked me what my major was and I responded it was a foreign language, the feedback was always the same. Many times these people questioned "What are you going to do with something like that?" accompanied with a frown on their faces. However, despite this somewhat negative attitude, I believe their opinions will soon be altered due to the fact that proficiency in foreign languages is becoming of utmost importance in today's society. Individuals possessing proficiency of this nature are in reality encountering numerous job opportunities. Many positions are available in government agencies requiring the knowledge of other languages beside English. Business firms frequently need to employ individuals with knowledge of foreign languages in the areas of public relations and foreign trade and finally, the health care industry needs individuals in order to treat foreign peoples in this country. One individual has summed up the job possibilities of bilingual individuals quite well . . . [lengthy quote which ends with this:] . . . there is one move you can make as a form of "insurance" for just about any career. Learn a foreign language.

Subject 1 develops the body of the paper with a discussion of foreign language careers in government, business, and health care, showing that there are numerous opportunities for employment for foreign language majors. In her discussion, she relies heavily on factual information, a strength of sensing writers described by Jensen and DiTiberio (173). She had also taken pains to compile a large amount of information on this issue, providing a list of ten sources on the Works Cited page, including several government documents, another feature of her work consistent with her type (156).

Four other students in the course read the paper: two sensing dominant, one feeling dominant, and one intuition dominant (see Figure 1). All four readers had positive responses to the paper, which was generally clear and was quite fully developed, even in its rough draft form. The two sensing dominant readers commented about a number of specific features of the paper, such as that it had "very few technical problems" and "good examples." One of these two pointed out that the paper begins in first person and "shifts to third person" and encouraged the writer to be more consistent. These kinds of comments are fairly typical of sensing dominant readers who attend to the practical realities of what is before them. One of the sensing dominant readers wrote these comments on the worksheet:

> There isn't a clear outline of the major portions that will be covered in the paper. . . . Rewrite thesis to outline major opportunities.

This response, asking as it does for the writer to set out more explicitly her plan for the paper, suggests that the sensing dominant reader wants a tangible statement of what the paper is going to take up and explore.

The two other readers of this paper also had positive reactions. In some ways, of course, reader responses on the worksheet are inevitably presented positively in an effort to spare the writers' feelings, but even so, the feeling dominant reader made these comments: "personal approach interesting . . . opening catches attention and discusses ideas coming up . . . content and examples are strong." In this case, the feeling dominant reader likes the feeling writer's choice to reach out and bring in the audience with the first few lines of the paper. The intuition dominant reader uses words that reflect to some degree his thinking function. The words that appear in his comments are "prove . . . state . . . argument . . . integration . . . coherency," all of which have to do with logic, reason, and the use of evidence. This reader also liked the use of examples to support the writer's point. In this first case, then, it is clear that the responders, while they are trying to be nice to the writer, all have specific reactions consistent with their personality types. Not surprisingly, the sensing and feeling dominant readers responded positively to this sensing-feeling writer's work. This first case, then, illustrates the situation when writer and readers share a dominant function and the good fit and high comprehension that results from the readable text among them.

Subject 2: Intuition dominant

Subject 2 is a non-traditional student whose type is ENFP (extraverted, intuitive, feeling and perceiving). Subject 2 already had full-time work experience and had returned to college to pursue his interest in computers. The opening paragraph of this paper reads as follows:

> Throughout my papers in . . . 101 I have investigated the possibility of becoming a systems analyst. I have examined in close detail the requirements of being a systems analyst. I have also looked at the possibility of owning my own small business. Each career deals with different aspects of computers, work place and lifestyles. There are advantages to each career. I know whether I choose to become a systems analyst or a small business owner, I will be successful in what I do.

Subject 2 proceeds to consider the nature of success and happiness, and in the course of this consideration, compares and contrasts systems analysis work with running a small computer consulting business from home. He also discusses what he likes about computers and how working with them is consistent with his personality type. From this, he proceeds to analyze the skills and abilities needed to work with computers in these two different settings and to see how well his present skills fit with these requirements. In the end, he summarizes the pros and cons of each choice and indicates that he will attempt to do both, pursuing experience needed to work as a systems analyst while developing the consulting business at the same time.

This draft is consistent with Jensen and DiTiberio's observations about intuitives as writers. This individual often asked about taking the assigned topics in his own direction, and he was happy to always be permitted to do so (174). The opening paragraph also fits with Jensen and DiTiberio's description of this preference as presenting

> generalities without examples. Their revisions may be more effective if they resolve the unnecessary complexities of their ideas [and] check their facts. . . . They tend to forget concrete examples and may not provide the reader with background information. (174)

Two readers of this paper are sensing dominant (see Figure 1). Both observe the inconsistency between the opening and the ending, and suggest that the writer should adjust the introduction. One tells the writer to "add that you will discuss computer market and your skills," while the other says, " . . . opening and ending not very consistent. I am convinced that computers are for him . . . but I don't believe that is what his thesis statement wants the reader to get." The first reader suggests this revision strategy:

> I would 1) state the fact that you're going to also discuss the computer market. Then 2) put the paragraphs dealing with the market and why you're good for the market first. Then narrow down to why those 2 careers are prime for you.

The second reader asks for more evidence and for some correction of technical points as well. These responses ask for a rather different approach and presentation than the intuition dominant writer is inclined to provide. That is, the sensing dominant readers ask for more specifics tied more closely to the realities of the world consistent with their preference, and different from the intuitive writer's theoretical discussion. As Jensen and DiTiberio point out, intuitive writers "excel at presenting theories and concepts and at devising new and unusual approaches to writing" (174). The sensing dominant readers, however, remind the writer of the need to be more specific and to tie his ideas more closely to the practical realities of his situation.

Even the feeling dominant third reader picks up on the inconsistency of the first paragraph with the rest of the paper. This reader notes: "Opening seems to decide between the two and the closing he is combining two different things." In written comments on a copy of the draft, this reader encourages the writer to move parts of the paper around to different positions in the discussion, and also asks for definitions of some technical terms (e.g., "bugs"). In this suggestion, the reader is telling the writer that he needs to reach out to readers, something a feeling dominant reader would be looking for that this intuition dominant writer does not provide. In this case, then, readers of different dominant types tell the intuition dominant writer clearly that he needs to make changes in his text to make his intentions more consistent with their expectations, given their various dominant types. As I have noted, it is painful to receive negative feedback on writing, but feedback like this that is informed by type theory can more easily be taken in the constructive spirit in which it is intended.

Subject 3: Thinking dominant

The third case is an instance of a traditional student whose type is ESTJ (extraverted, sensing, thinking and judging). According to his paper, he wants to be in politics and has used the paper to explore possible college majors that will help him reach his career goal. Here is the opening paragraph of Subject 3's research paper:

> Most Americans are interested in politics and hold some form of a political opinion. If nothing else, it gives them something to complain about because they can always do a better job. This leadership quality, which encompasses the career of politics, is what draws me towards a political career. Since fifth grade, I haven't been able to shake this fascination with the subject. The many unanswered questions I have accumulated over the years are clouding my vision of a career path. What should I be studying ... Law? Political Science? Business? How does a person run for office and what happens after the election? Having a business background can obviously be a great asset, but other factors do need to be considered before making this occupational choice.

The draft version of the paper is developed through the presentation of three interviews with local politicians in Subject 3's community, and discussion of practical aspects of holding office. In the end, he remains uncertain of a choice of major and is aware that a political career has many problems and difficulties despite the rewards he seeks and feels capable of attaining. Thus, in some ways, Subject 3's approach is aptly described by Jensen and DiTiberio, who comment on the work of thinking writers this way:

> In their introductions, they often establish a point of view and then argue against it. . . . While writing they tend to focus on the content rather than how the material is presented to the audience. . . . In revising, they may need to enliven their writing with some personal examples and qualify blunt statements. (174)

The responses to Subject 3's paper from his readers all suggest that this description characterizes his work, especially the third reader who provided him with a very rich response.

Subject 3 got a range of feedback from his three readers, one sensing dominant, one thinking dominant (like himself), and one feeling dominant (see Figure 1). The sensing dominant reader got his message clearly and comments on his apparent confusion and inability to reach a decision about his future. Though she provides few comments, she does note that Subject 3 used many contractions in his writing and may have been suggesting that he try to make the tone more formal. As noted in the first case, this is a typical reaction of sensing types. The thinking dominant reader is also a sensing type, and comments on the contractions, along with a suggestion that he make his thesis "more specific and talk about politicians and the business field more." She asks for more details and description, a reasonable request since he notes at various points in the draft his intention to add to the text. These two readers show Subject 3 a need to attend more closely to how he says what he says, as well as a need for more evidence to develop his point more fully.

The third reader of this paper provided the most interesting response because in addition to responding to the points raised on the standard worksheet, she also chose to write detailed comments on the copy of the draft itself. These comments depart from the issues that require attention raised by the worksheet points. The reader is feeling dominant and is also an intuitive type. She comments on the worksheet that from the opening she has some expectations that are not met by the paper, that it will take up pros and cons of a political career and "some behind the scenes things" that she doesn't seem to think are delivered in the body. She sympathizes with his confusion, saying "he seems to have a feel for it, but isn't sure what it takes and where it leads to." One specific revision suggestion asks him to explain more about the development of a bill that he uses as an example "because if everyone is like me, they are politically illiterate." This comment is an instance of the reader asking the writer for more connection, a common request for a feeling dominant individual who values human connection more than anything else. It is also consistent with the kind of revising Jensen and DiTiberio suggest is needed by thinking writers (174), that is, qualifying blunt statements and fleshing out examples.

This reader wrote detailed notes on four of the six pages of the draft. Most of her comments ask for further explanation, with notes like "maybe tell a little more" and "I'm lost" and "I know it's obvious why, but write it anyway to blend with the rest." Such comments say to the writer, in effect, "give more information, reach out to me as a reader and give me some ways to connect to your ideas." At the end, she summarizes her notes by saying this:

It's a good paper. Some places, you should probably elaborate and you need another page. But don't worry about telling too much. You have a way of writing that makes this interesting, so don't cut things short—give us the whole bloody mess!!

It seems clear that this reader is willing to reach out to connect with the writer, but Subject 3 hasn't given her enough to go on to make the connection. This feeling dominant reader has expectations that the thinking dominant writer has not fulfilled. This case shows that thinking writers can benefit significantly from feedback of readers whose dominant is opposite their own.

Subject 4: Feeling dominant

The final case involves a writer who is feeling dominant, a student of traditional age. Subject 4's type is ESFJ (extraverted, sensing, feeling and judging). Although not a first-year student when she took the course, she had changed majors and schools a few times and seemed to make good use of the assignment to explore an aspect of her current career choice. Here is the opening paragraph of her research paper:

> Scandalous stories about Hollywood fill our newspapers, magazines and television shows. Devoted followers love to share gossip involving the romance and personal lives of stars. This enchantment towards performers helps to make the entertainment industry a booming business. Careers in this field seem to be highly contagious within families. Only one member needs to catch "an interest in entertainment".[sic] Then, like a nasty flu virus, it spreads, often infecting the entire family. While some relatives work independently within the industry, many families choose careers which allow them to work in entertainment together. Entertaining, a high energy outlet, offers families the opportunity to spend time together in an exciting atmosphere, usually with an appreciative audience. However, behind the glamour of performing are the mundane, yet important jobs necessary to maintain a successful business. This everyday work with family often causes conflicts among the family members. Combining family and business complicates the interrelated relationships. As a partner in a new family business, I witness and participate in many family feuds. Working with relatives creates new roles, often changing expectations and behavior. In addition, specialists agree the greatest problem in family business relationships is lack of communication. Communication problems and relationship changes cause conflicts when working with relatives.

In this lengthy opening, Subject 4 attempts to make clear the reason for her interest in this area, and points the way toward the rest of the paper in which she discusses the problems of communication within families who work together in an entertainment business. In the development, her analysis proceeds to review several aspects of flawed communication, moving back and forth from experts' analyses of problems and solutions for communication difficulties in family business to personal examples from the business she is in with her parents and brothers. The paper might be described as being about relationships, summarized by the first sentence of the closing paragraph: "Working with relatives requires an understanding of the possible relationship changes and communication problems."

Following Jensen and DiTiberio's analysis, this writer offers an opening and focus on a topic which reflects her dominant feeling preference. They write:

> Feeling types prefer topics that they can care about . . . deciding how a writing project is of value to them is an important part of their prewriting phase. While writing, they tend to draw upon personal experience. . . . Feeling types tend to excel at topics that draw upon feelings, and thus are good at making contact with the audience. They qualify their statements, but their writing will usually reflect a deep personal conviction. Their writing often contains personal examples and reflects a concern to make their writing interesting. (175)

Subject 4's paper makes much use of her experiences in a family business, drawing strongly on her natural inclinations as described by Jensen and DiTiberio.

The three readers of this paper include two who are sensing dominant with thinking as a second function, and a third who is also sensing dominant, but with feeling as a second function (see Figure 1). Their responses are quite consistent with one another and indicate their different expectations and need for more concrete information than Subject 4 provides. Of the two sensing-thinking readers, one suggests that the "[t]hesis could state the major points in a more definite manner," while the other finds the opening a little misleading and suggests she "could get rid of the first part of the intro that talks about entertainment and Hollywood stars." The third reader, who is sensing dominant, but also a feeling type, finds the paper convincing because the writer "has explained well the problems of a family working together. I think her personal insight gives strength to the paper because she has hands on experience." Also true to type, two of these readers commented on technical points, a kind of issue sensing types are likely to notice with their practical focus on the here-and-now. In this fourth case, readers are once again helpful in showing this feeling writer how to enhance a readable text through responses consistent with their various dominant types.

These cases have been chosen to illustrate how each of the four possible dominant functions can be significant to how writers present their ideas, and how readers respond based on their own preferences and especially their dominant functions. The ways that each dominant type tends to present ideas in writing and the ways that readers in each dominant type respond to a text are summarized in Figure 2.

Figure 2. Dominant types as writers and readers.

Sensing dominant writers: Rely on facts, details; have many sources, usually technically correct.	*Sensing dominant readers want:* Practical reality, technical correctness, outline, consistent opening and ending, order.
Intuitive dominant writers: Go in their own direction; give generalities, few facts, examples or specifics; offer strong theoretical discussion.	*Intuitive dominant readers want:* Integration, patterns, overview.
Thinking dominant writers: Focus on content, not reader reaction or connection; make blunt statements; offer few examples.	*Thinking dominant readers want:* Proof, argument, logical organization; concrete information.
Feeling dominant writers: Write about topics they care about and personal values; use personal experience; connect with readers.	*Feeling dominant readers want:* Personal approach; connection of reader and writer; like expectations to be met.

It is important to keep in mind that no type is "right" or more right than another, but that each type has a contribution to make; in reading/writing transactions in texts, the cases discussed here show that each individual works from a particular frame of reference shaped by personality preferences. Readers can get more of what writers have to offer when they share dominant preferences, but since this is unlikely as a consistent and practical matter, there is a clear message for writers: texts need to be shaped to appeal both to writers' own preferences and to the differing preferences of potential readers so that they can get meaning from the text. When writers provide texts that are accessible for not only readers who share their preferences but also readers from the opposite end of each dimension, readable texts result.

The cases examined here within the framework of personality type theory and Jensen and DiTiberio's understanding of how writers display their preferences in text support the essential role of personality preferences in literacy and in the reader/writer transactions of readable text: the most readable kinds of discourse are those in which writers have made an effort to balance the text in terms of both their own and the readers' personalities. Readable text must draw on all the dimensions of personality type. The case studies show that when readers and writers have a good fit in terms of personality preferences, texts are more readable. Where this fit is lacking, writers can profit from readers' feedback to address the needs of different dominant types. These findings can enrich our understanding of text processing in reading and writing because they clarify why writers present their ideas in certain ways and why readers respond as they do. With this understanding we can achieve the much needed critical literacy among our citizens by enabling writers to meet readers in readable text.

Works Cited

Horning, Alice S. *The Psycholinguistics of Readable Writing: A Multidisciplinary Exploration.* Norwood, NJ: Ablex, 1993.

Jensen, George, and John DiTiberio. *Personality and the Teaching of Composition.* Norwood, NJ: Ablex, 1989.

Jung, Carl G. *Psychological Types.* Trans. H. G. Baynes. Trans. revised by R. F. C. Hull. Princeton, NJ: Princeton U P, 1971. Trans. of *Psychologische Typen.* Zurich: Rasher Verlag, 1921.

Pittenger, David J. "Measuring the MBTI . . . And Coming Up Short." *Journal of Career Planning and Employment* 54.1 (1993): 48–52.

Scribner, Sylvia, and Michael Cole. *The Psychology of Literacy.* Cambridge, MA: Harvard U P, 1981.

Singer, Marti. "Cognitive Style and Reading Comprehension." *Journal of Psychological Type* 17 (1989): 31–35.

Smith, Frank. *Writing and the Writer.* New York: Holt, 1982.

6   Personality Preferences and Responding to Student Writing

Jane Bowman Smith

Two familiar stories demonstrate many students' views of evaluation. The first: "She just throws the papers down the stairs—the ones that make it to the bottom get A's." The second is usually told to the teacher directly: "I know you gave me a C—but Ms. Wilson told me she'd have given this at least a B+." The currency of stories like these should not be surprising. While some subjects may be evaluated purely objectively, the grading of writing is subjective, despite ongoing attempts in composition research to determine what objective grading is, or whether it can even exist. Teachers continue to disagree in grading sessions, in departmental meetings, and at professional conferences as they attempt to define excellent—and failing— student writing.

Understanding why evaluation is so subjective begins with a realization of the process's complexity. Little has been written about what actually happens in teachers' minds as they read and evaluate their students' writing. But simply put, the process of evaluation has three phases: 1) the teacher reads the student's paper and gathers the information used to answer at least these three questions: what does the student know?, what does the student need to learn?, and how effective is the paper as a response to the assignment?; 2) the teacher decides what merits response, either orally or in writing, then makes both formative and summative comments; and 3) the teacher assigns a grade and may record information about the paper which will be used later to note the student's progress.

While all teachers go through these three steps in some form when grading—perhaps not always as purposively as they might!—individual teachers handle the process very differently from one another. Education and training, time constraints, and departmental conventions can affect the individual teacher's responding style. Personality type can also affect the entire evaluative process, both in the method and techniques used when grading and in what one values or disparages in student writing.

The following discussion suggests how the four indices—EI, SN, TF, and JP—can affect the way a teacher responds to and evaluates a student's paper. Obviously, however, personality type cannot and does not "control" what a teacher does in the classroom; people are, above all, individuals. Personality theory does offer a construct, however, for creating a procedure that enables teachers to individualize their instruction. Throughout this discussion, I will make use of the commentary of two instructors, Sam and Cathy, who are "opposites" in terms of their personality types. Sam, an INTP, and Cathy, an ESFJ, grade very differently from one another, not only in terms of the grading situation that each has created, but also in their responses to student writing and their commentary. Their comments suggest how each dimension is actually part of a complex whole: the individual teacher's response to student writing.

Extraversion

The extraverted teacher looks forward to a discussion of ideas, as talking is often a means of thinking for the extravert, and may design the grading situation to allow for conferencing and intervention during the process. Cathy, an ESFJ, reports that she uses talk "to work [her] way through a writing block and rebuild [her] enthusiasm." She uses this technique in class with her students to keep them motivated through the revision process: "although I have to remember," she says, "to listen to the students—and not talk them to death myself!" An extravert may also be comfortable with conference grading, which allows the student and teacher to talk, negotiating both the revision process and the grade. Extraverts also prefer experience to reflection, and so may want to "leap" into the grading, perhaps writing a series of comments down the margins, rather than waiting until they've finished reading and then mulling over the strengths and weaknesses of the text. Cathy remarks that her style of grading, an ongoing commentary on the text as she reads, is "almost like freewriting—the closest kind of writing to talk." Sometimes the immediacy of her responding style gets her "into trouble," she comments, when her "first reactions contradict the ones later in the paper."

Extraverts may respond better to a paper when the content is broadly explorative; they may be more interested in papers that demonstrate "initiative" and a student's clear engagement with the world. Cathy, for example, expects her students "to deal with the real world in their writing and [wants] to see how their research can be put to use." This response, of course, may hurt a student who is more interested in pure research or theory.

Introversion

Because introverted teachers need time to reflect, they will be more likely to set up the grading situation so that they read and think about their students' writing privately. Sam, an INTP, finds himself reading the paper and imagining the student's responses to his commentary in his head; he has to "remind [himself] that the student won't know that we had this 'conversation'!" They are less likely than extraverts to use techniques that demand they read and then discuss the paper with the student immediately, without mental preparation. If an introverted teacher does arrange conferences with the students, he or she may ask students to hand in notes, a plan, etc. before the conference so the teacher can prepare. Sam does conference regularly with his students because he knows they find it useful; he reports, however, that he finds himself "staring off into space" to think through his response; "this," he says, "disconcerts students until they get to know me."

Introverted teachers are willing to concentrate on a student's paper and think deeply about it—a clear strength; however, many techniques that are useful to students, notably those that demand the teacher intervene in the process to help the student improve the paper, are sometimes avoided by introverted teachers. In terms of a paper's content, introverts value depth, development, and introspection, often about a single idea. They appreciate a focused, thoughtfully developed paper, while a broad topic may be criticized as "too general" or "shallow." Sam was embarrassed to discover, after he looked over several semesters of student work, that students who had written papers in which they related several humorous experiences— their purpose being to entertain—received lower grades than they probably deserved.

Sensing

The preference for sensing or intuition strongly affects the way teachers respond to student writing because it influences the kind of information the person selects to "take in." Sensing teachers will generally want a practical, realistic way to grade their students' papers and will work patiently with the "routine" of grading because they value accuracy and consistency. Cathy claims "never to procrastinate. I'd rather grade the papers than think about doing it!" Sensing teachers also tend to provide precise directions about what to do and what they are looking for. Because sensing types in general are particularly aware of details, they often design or prefer grading strategies that respond to the text at the sentence level. Cathy says that she finds it satisfying to make use of techniques such as checklists to follow when evaluating.

The sensing teacher will tend to read and attend to the actual text itself as a rhetorical structure and evaluate what is there rather than making inferences; when they are deciding what grade to give, they are attentive to the student's clarity, accuracy, factual support, and attention to mechanics. It irritates Cathy when "students don't seem to care about the appearance of a final draft—when they don't proofread carefully or haven't corrected errors that were pointed out in class." They are generally better than intuitive teachers at refining the concrete text; their evaluation may reflect their sense of the student's concern for careful research, details and supporting evidence, and organization (especially if they are also thinking types). Cathy, for example, "[attends] to the details first to use them as a starting point for the ideas that tie the paper together." Sensing teachers prefer to keep careful records of student progress, especially if they are also judging types. Particularly if the sensing teacher comments primarily about sentence level errors, students can infer that their content—what they have to say, their meaning—is not important to the teacher. For a particularly sensitive student, a teacher's exclusive focus on errors may lead to writing anxiety.

Intuition

Intuitives prefer to use their imaginations both to create their grading situation and as they read a text; resisting routines, they may redesign their grading rubric or try new approaches to grade more efficiently or fairly. This may confuse those students who expect consistency. Intuitive teachers tend to be more interested in what they can infer from what they read than in the actual text itself, imagining the writer's intentions. This can be valuable to students who do not know how to develop their ideas or are uncertain that they have anything to say. However, Sam finds writing that is extremely concrete and detailed "boring, especially if it doesn't make a point of some kind" and may assign a lower grade, especially if he cannot imagine "where the paper is going."

Intuitive types also tend to give directions differently than sensing types: while sensing teachers' directions tend to be very specific, intuitives tend to give more general directions. Sam is annoyed by students who "ask me how long the paper should be, or whether they have to write a summary conclusion. I can't tell them what to do until I see what they've got in rough draft form." Intuitives can also misread a student's intentions, which may result in directions that bewilder students who don't understand what the teacher saw in their papers. Although this way of looking at student writing allows for flexibility, it can also be unfair to the student if the teacher controls the writing's future direction.

In terms of comments, intuitive types may be better at suggesting how the student can write a better paper next time; they will deal with the ideas, the "global issues" of the paper, first, and worry about surface errors at a later stage in the process. Sam reports, for example, that he tends to "read over" local problems, as with spelling, unconsciously correcting them mentally as he gets involved in the student's ideas. Because intuitives value abstractions and conceptualizations, they tend to prefer student writing which is theoretical, even when this is at the expense of careful documentation. Thus, the potential weaknesses of a typical intuitive teacher's response are that it can imply that the teacher does not care about errors or isn't "doing the job" of evaluating, and that it can deal so much with the paper's potential that the actual text is lost.

Thinking

Whether a teacher has a thinking or feeling preference profoundly influences the way he or she grades. Thinking types tend not to see their evaluation as "personal"; they see evaluation more objectively, a process that should be focused on the student's writing and not on the student as an individual. Committed to problem-solving, thinking teachers will analyze student writing as they read, hoping to discover ways to help the students solve their writing difficulties. They are often focused on their students' learning rather than on their personal relationships with students. Sam's goal is "to be consistent when I grade and to encourage all the students to meet my standards." Thinking types prefer to have established criteria to use in the decision-making process and often give these to students in advance.

Thinking types also tend to believe students want and need criticism in order to learn, and this motivates their comments. They tend to prefer a symmetrical structure in writing that shows how idea and detail are logically related. When reading papers, they look for evidence of logic and objective thought. Their comments are worded in terms of problem-solving advice; they ignore their personal feelings for the student in a way that is difficult for feeling types. Sam, unlike Cathy, must remind himself to find things to praise legitimately; he also "dislikes to waste time in explaining the obvious." Thinking types are less interested than feeling types in personal details, which they may see as irrelevant or sentimental, and distrust what they see as a writer's overconcern with audience.

A thinking teacher's response may be too critical or too focused on the problems in a student's writing; like Sam, thinking types may find it hard to praise. Another potential weakness is the tendency to use a "yes, BUT . . ." statement, in which criticism undercuts the compliment.

Feeling

Feeling types often dread grading because of the potential to hurt or disappoint the student. This is itself a weakness that can lead to more subjective grading if a teacher weakens necessary criticism. Cathy is very aware that she tends "to be too sympathetic when a student claims to have tried hard or has learned something." Like many FJ types, she prefers to consider the particular situation. Her natural response is to empathize with students and "nurture" them, and she admits that she has to "watch that reaction." Feeling types often prefer to avoid making hard decisions. The opposite can be true, however, when the feeling teacher gets tired and impatient at the end of the term: Cathy finds herself "getting really angry at students who seem to ignore my suggestions over and over. I have to resist the impulse to 'get back at them' with their grades!"

In terms of content, feeling types tend to value personal examples and voice, the sense that the writer is involved in the text and is reaching out to the audience. Because they are more convinced by personal examples and emotional appeal, they will tend to find purely logical or objective writing, particularly when supported by data that leave out the "human touch," as less "interesting"—a buzzword for feeling types—and possibly grade it more harshly.

Once they begin marking a student's writing, feeling types will be aware of their commentary's potential effect on the student. Their commentary tends to support the relationship that exists between teacher and student, because they often believe a personal relationship is motivating. Thus, they praise students for work well done, may suggest or question rather than give directions, and tend to let the writer know how the text affected them. Finally, they tend to explain things they mark on the paper; rather than simply correct an error, they will explain the rule. They tend to value self-expressive writing, especially if it has a clear voice, and to view it as more mature.

The weaknesses of feeling types lie in the tendency to soften criticism and to be too involved in their own personal response to the content rather than to the objective achievements and failures of the writing; also, their emotional involvement in the grading process can be problematic.

Judging

Judging teachers, with their tendency to exclude information and their desire to make decisions efficiently, often prefer a systematized approach to grading, especially if they are also sensing types. Judging types may read a few paragraphs and decide that the paper is probably a "C"; further reading will be seen as a means to confirm their hypothesis. In general, judging types believe they are "right," and they sometimes find it difficult to see another's point of view. Cathy examines the first paragraph of a paper "to know where the paper is going and to enjoy the student's plan." She admits that she will then lower the grade if the student does not follow the plan established in the first paragraph. To her, the first paragraph creates a "contract" between the writer and the reader. A potential weakness that results from such decisiveness is the corresponding dislike of ambiguity in student writing; judging teachers may create a mental outline of the student's paper and lower the grade if the writing strays from the plan. Although Cathy resented teachers who "told her exactly what to do, [she] still [finds herself] using a 'my way or no way!' approach."

In evaluating the essay, the judging teacher may prefer writing with an obvious conclusion (a decision was made) rather than something too speculative or open-ended. The desire to finish the task—in this case, grading papers—may also prompt judging types to ignore or simply not see the good in an unusual approach to an assignment. Because they naturally limit their topics in writing, excluding what they see as unnecessary information, they may find this skill difficult to teach. They may find it easier to teach students to develop their ideas, as this was something they had to learn themselves.

Judging teachers, because of their generally orderly approach to life and their teaching, will be more likely than perceiving teachers to keep notes on their students' progress. However, their tendency to rely on established plans may make them resistant to change, even when their system needs an overhaul.

Perceiving

Because perceiving types tend to value thoroughness over decisiveness, they often prefer to read their students' work comprehensively. Sam has no trouble reading a student paper completely through before marking on it. Further, they want to share their perceptions of the text rather than to make a judgment about it; however, the grading situation forces them to assign a grade, which is a judgment. Because they prefer spontaneity, they resist a set routing for grading; Sam, in fact, doesn't keep a grade book. He records his students' names and the grades for the papers he is marking on separate sheets of paper for each assignment as he goes along, noting down stray bits of information that seem important at the time. (At the end of the semester, he collects and tabulates all these sheets, reading and considering all the information before recording the students' final grades for the class.) Although few perceiving types are this spontaneous, many have to be convinced that a departmental "grading standard" will really benefit the students, because they see it as a restriction on their preferred, open-ended evaluation style. And it will probably be a judging type, not a perceiving type, who originally felt a need for the standard.

In terms of the paper's content, perceiving types tend to value speculation and prefer exploration of the subject to resolutions about it. Unlike judging types, they are likely to enjoy the unexpected, and thus tend to be more open to an unusual approach to an assignment. Perceiving types also tend to be more involved in a student's process of writing the text, again because of their preference for exploration. Perceiving teachers find it harder to deal with judging students who need to be taught to explore and to develop their topics; they work more easily with perceiving students like themselves, who need to learn to restrict their topics and organize their writing. Finally, because they are so adaptive, they may be less willing to provide clear directions for improvement, and may prefer to share their perception about the students' papers. Students may be unable to use these perceptions as a guide for revision.

Summary of Preferences

Extraverts like:
- to talk with students about their papers
- to make evaluation "immediate"
- content that is explorative and deals with the "real world"

Introverts like:
- to reflect in privacy while grading
- to think carefully before commenting
- content that is developed and deals with the "inner world" of ideas

Sensing types like:
- practical ways to grade; a routine
- to deal with the paper that's there
- papers that are accurate, detailed, and mechanically clean
- checklists

Intuitive types like:
- to experiment with new means of grading
- to deal with the paper that could be
- papers that speculate or are highly theoretical
- global or holistic comments on student progress

Thinking types like:
- to see evaluation as logical and objective
- to grade consistently and uniformly
- to identify and offer solutions to the writer's problems
- content and structure to be orderly and logical

Feeling types like:
- to see evaluation as motivating
- to grade based on individual effort and achievement
- to use comments to motivate the students to learn
- content that is personal and writing that has a voice

Judging types like:
- to grade in an efficient way
- writing that is clearly "to the point" and decisive
- to maintain their grading system or record- keeping plan (resist change)

Perceiving types like:
- to grade thoroughly
- content that is speculative and explores the subject
- to be involved in their students' ongoing process rather than products

Although the chart above is "neat" and appears authoritative, nobody can be reduced to a place on a chart. As has been explained in other chapters of this book, a person is also much more than a "combination" of four preferences, and this is true for how teachers grade, as well. Cathy's grading style is not simply the result of all the separate characteristics listed above for E + S + F + J. At least three other influences are in operation here; two relate to personality theory. First, preferences interact. Cathy's strong preference for feeling judgment would be manifested differently if she were an ENFJ. She would still want to praise her students to motivate them, but she would tend to comment more on their ideas and the potential she saw in their texts than in the details and clarity of their writing. Second, individuals may have stronger or lesser degrees of preference. Sam is much more strongly introverted than is David, who is also an INTP. He is much more likely than Sam to use group work in class and talk informally with students about their writing difficulties in a class workshop session.

Although personality type offers insights into teachers' evaluation practices, it is not the only influence. Departmental standards—particularly when they have been carefully thought out to reach a balance among composing and writing styles—and teacher training that has dealt with these same issues, may actually influence teachers more than their personality types. However, type bias does exist. So, how can a teacher avoid this particular kind of subjective grading, a subjectivity which is influenced by personality type?

Achieving Balance

Understanding that one's preferences can affect how one grades is an important first step. Teachers who are familiar with personality theory will understand that one's type affects both the way one prefers to grade and also the kinds of writing that are particularly appealing. This understanding is the first step toward creating a more individualized responding style that supports all types as the students mature as writers.

Another important problem to be considered is the impact these grading preferences have on students. If Cathy has a class of ESFJs, like herself, they will clearly benefit insofar that her natural preferences—what she herself tends to do when she writes—will also appear in her students' writing. Further, she will teach them what she herself has had to learn as she has matured as a writer. The students will also probably understand her comments and her style of responding. If Sam has this same class of ESFJs, however, neither the students nor Sam will be completely pleased with the outcome. Sam will probably be looking for a very different style of writing—and his comments may confuse or frustrate his students.

Achieving a balanced responding style demands an awareness of oneself and one's pedagogical practices. Following are suggestions for moving in the direction of balance:

- discuss grading styles and preferences with others, especially with those who are not of your type;
- evaluate student papers with a group of colleagues and discuss similarities and differences;
- examine papers that you graded in the past, as well as your rubrics, checklists, etc. for examples of type bias.

Finally, an awareness of the inherent weaknesses of your own preferences can lead to correction: remember the strengths of the opposing preference. A thinking type might be better at identifying problems, but can learn from a feeling colleague's ability to praise. Ultimately, students will benefit from these efforts.

7   Working with Individual Differences in the Writing Tutorial

Muriel Harris

Because new composition teachers and new writing center tutors tend to focus on themselves—conscientiously worrying about their own abilities to help writers—they need to be reminded that an equally important part of their preparation is learning to recognize how different each of their students will be. Becoming aware of differences among writers is not something normally high on a new teacher or tutor's list of priorities because we tend to think of writers in groups. Writers can be categorized as freshmen or sophomores or as basic writers and more advanced writers and so on, but we generally don't focus on the individuality of every writer—at first. This may be because the classroom is an environment that is set up to work with groups. But the writing center tutorial—like a teacher's conferences with each of her students—is by its nature a one-to-one interaction. It is here that we can recognize, honor, and work with individual differences. But new teachers and tutors need some help in seeing all the different trees in the forest, in realizing how different writers can be from each other. That is, when a teacher or tutor meets one-to-one with a student, there are two people coming together from very different worlds. The teacher/tutor and student each have a different set of perspectives, as well as a different history, set of concerns, skill levels, and priorities. And they each have different internal make-ups, different ways of perceiving and interacting with the world around them. But they can meet and work together productively, and by recognizing differences, they can work even more effectively.

Recognizing differences and learning to work with those differences is particularly important in the one-to-one setting of a conference, either between a teacher and a student or in a writing center tutorial, because the teacher or tutor is working with the student's language processing abilities, an area where personal differences exert great influence. We write and think about writing in a variety of ways that reflect our differences, and for those of us who are teachers or tutors or who are preparing ourselves to fill those roles, we need to be aware of factors that influence both how we talk to students as well as how we talk about writing with them. Writing center theory particularly emphasizes the collaborative nature of this talk when tutor and student work together. But while the tutor and student may be discussing the student's paper, the tutor also recognizes that her larger goal is to help the writer become a better writer, not to fix the paper that brought the student to the writing center. It is necessary, therefore, for the tutor to keep firmly in mind that it is the student, not the paper, which is the object of improvement.

The same theory also stresses the importance of providing personalized, individual help so that when we say that the tutor's goal is to help the writer gain more mastery over writing processes, we mean that particular student's writing processes, not some abstract concept of whatever constitutes the act of writing. Thus, for example, when a student comes to the Writing Lab where I tutor, it often helps us to begin by chatting about how the student wrote the paper she has brought along. Our job, as tutors, is to listen for signs that the writer has effective strategies for planning, drafting, revising, and editing; and we ask about any problems she had in getting that draft on paper. We must not and cannot offer generic answers to her questions; and we must not and cannot engage in collaborative discussion and question-asking which is so generic that it doesn't matter who is sitting there with us. Being on auto-pilot is a dangerous error for a writing tutor because the pedagogical goal of a writing center tutor is to work with the particular student sitting there, to help in whatever way that writer needs help. Tutor preparation therefore needs to include some training in the ways that people can differ as well as the ways in which such differences affect both writing and the instructional conversation of a writing teacher or tutor and the writer.

There are a number of ways to identify various dimensions of individual differences, but the MBTI is one that I have found particularly useful. My purpose here is to describe how personality preferences can affect the writing conference, and I'll do so in terms of describing how I train tutors to become aware of such differences and to recognize how this knowledge can be used in tutorials. Since my experience is primarily in writing centers, I will draw on that experience—particularly in terms of how the MBTI can be introduced in tutor training as well as how it can affect the tutoring process. But teachers who conference with their students about writing will quickly see how relevant a knowledge of personality preferences can be to them when they meet one-to-one with their students.

Differences in Writing Processes

Of the semester-long list of topics introduced in the tutor training courses I teach, type theory is one that produces some of the most lively discussion and is often mentioned in end-of-the-semester evaluations as one of the most useful areas of preparation in the course. The tutors begin by looking at themselves and how their responses to the MBTI correlate with the ways they write. The initial emphasis in such discussions is on differences between writers and how they write, and for some tutors it is their first awareness that not all of us write in the same way. Many begin with the notion that there is only one way to write or that advice they have read in books or been told in a composition class is the only correct way to proceed. (For a discussion of this idea, see my chapter "Don't Believe Everything You're Taught: Matching Writing Processes and Personal Preferences" in Wendy Bishop's book for students, *The Subject Is Writing*.)

The usefulness of the tutors' new awareness of differences in writing processes becomes apparent when we tease out how such differences affect tutorial collaboration. We begin with a discussion of our own writing processes and then talk about some intersections with the type preferences described in the MBTI. Initially, the tutors find it fascinating to hear from some members of the class who say that they begin with a great deal of planning in their heads. Others in the class note that they have to grab some paper or turn on their computers and write for awhile to see where they are going. Some say they like to start sharing what they have with another reader; others express great reluctance to show their writing until it is further along. Some say that while they listen to what another person says about their draft, they then prefer to go somewhere quiet and work it out by themselves. Others operate well by doing some revising while in the midst of a discussion with their reader. There's usually at least one person in the group who says she needs an outline before she can write, while another student insists that she can't even think about an outline until she has at least a rough draft started. Sometimes we have someone in a class who says that he has to have a perfect first sentence before he can go on. That might provoke another person to respond that she generally tosses away a couple of first drafts before she gets down to really tackling the assignment. Some of the class note that they place great value on getting the details right while others talk about reaching for the big ideas and hoping the details get in there somehow, sometime. They talk about whether they are aware of their readers while writing. They compare differences in whether they are comfortable with continual revising until the paper is due or whether they find that when they are done with a draft, they are done and can't go back and revise any more.

Eventually, I move this discussion on to personality types. Having read about these types and taken the MBTI, the tutors are ready to make connections between different ways to write and different personality preferences. Such discussion begins to expand the tutors' horizons. They can see their own writing strengths and weaknesses a bit more clearly and recognize what they have to watch for. Then with some questioning on my part, they begin to see why students with whom they will be working will approach both the tutorial and their writing in ways that might look either very familiar or very different to the tutor. When one member of the class says, "So I guess that I shouldn't always tell my students to start with an outline," I know that the discussion of type preferences, coupled with one about their writing processes, has raised their levels of awareness in how to work with individual differences in writing and learning to write. As Carolina, a student in one of my recent tutor-training classes, notes: "I had never thought about the importance of personality types in terms of the tutorial, but it's only logical. There are two people, face to face—one trying to help, the other wanting or not wanting to be helped. I have to admit that up until now I had very egocentric thinking in that I thought most people write the same way I do." Beth adds: "I thought I had figured out how to write good papers. I suppose I see now that what I've really figured out is how I should write them." This does not mean that tutors can't share their strategies with their students, but they have to do so with the awareness that such strategies may or may not help, depending on how similar the student is to them. In short, descriptions of writing strategies become suggestions, not instructions.

Tutorials that Focus on Planning

While type theory helps us explore differences in writing styles, it also suggests some of the differences in the ways people interact because of personality preferences. This is particularly important for tutors because the tutorial itself will be shaped by the personalities of those two people working elbow to elbow. Perhaps the easiest to note is the influence of personality preferences on the planning conversation that frequently is the main focus of a writing center tutorial. Students often come to writing centers to talk with a tutor before they begin writing. Tutorial talk can be an energizing planning experience, and tutors learn to ask the kinds of questions that will help the writer begin brainstorming and generating material for writing the paper. Tutors need to recognize that sometimes such planning sessions seem to go particularly well, especially when both tutor and student are extraverts. The talk flows freely, and the tutors' questions seem to lead the writer to explore avenues of thought that appear fruitful. At the end of the tutorial, the tutor and writer are likely to part feeling that they've had a great session together.

By comparison other tutorials seem quieter. The tutor talks, and the student listens but adds less to the conversation. Extraverted tutors need to recognize that the quieter tutorial is not necessarily a less successful tutorial, nor should the tutor expect the student to write or take notes during the tutorial. In such cases, it may be that the student is more of an introvert, listening carefully so that she can think about it all later and write in her preferred style when she is alone. Both may have been very successful tutorials, but the extraverted tutor may feel defeated or discouraged by the reduction in the sheer volume of talk. Or the tutor may not recognize that a useful thing to do would be to leave the more introverted student alone after some tutorial conversation so that the student can begin to write, something an introvert may be less likely to do during the conversational flow of the tutorial. Extraverted tutors also need to heed the description of extraverts in action offered by George Jensen and John DiTiberio: "In conversations, extraverts are more likely to initiate the topics being discussed, alter the direction of the discussion, and interrupt other speakers. For them, an interruption is an integral part of conversations" (9). Even though as tutors we work on the basis that the tutor should never monopolize or dominate the conversation, for the quieter student, trying to get a word in edgewise may be a difficult maneuver. Similarly, the quieter tutor working with a more extraverted student has to make a conscious effort to converse in ways with which the student will feel comfortable. The danger is that an extraverted student might take the silence from the introvert tutor as a sign of disinterest or an indication that what she is saying has little merit.

It is not necessary that we ask every student who enters the writing center to complete an MBTI; it is necessary only that the tutor remember that each student who sits down at the table will not respond in the same manner as the previous student. Tutors in training classes inevitably ask how they will know what to do. Eventually, after some experience with tutoring, they begin to realize that what they are doing is trying out some possibilities, based on whatever quick mental appraisals they can do about the person they are sitting with. "Go with what you think may be right for that student, " says Ed, one of our more experienced tutors. "When it flops, you move to your next option," he adds. My advice at that point is to phrase each possible tutorial move or strategy as a question for the student to decide. For example, if the student is relatively subdued and seems to be listening without taking notes, we can ask after there has been an adequate amount of time spent on planning discussion, "Would you like to sit here for a bit now and do some writing while I move to another tutoring table, or would you rather continue talking?" Students are often ready to tell us what the most appropriate next step is for them. In response to such a question, I've had students glance at me nervously and comment, "I'm not sure where I'm going with this paper yet." That's a clue that I should stay where I am and that we should continue talking. But when someone looks decidedly relieved and says, "Yeah, I think I need to sort this out by myself," I know it's time for me to get up and move away, thereby permitting that student to have some quiet time by himself. "I'll be here in the room," I explain. "Let me know if and when I should come back and continue our conversation." (As an extravert, I have to recognize that my temptation is to stay there and keep talking, and I need to make a conscious effort to cease all the conversation that I see as so productive.)

There are other factors to watch for in the planning conversation of some tutorials. There are students who use that time to spin endless streams of ideas. They seem reluctant to get down to choosing a topic and the direction in which they will take it. Sometimes this can signal a student's personality preference for perceiving. Such a writer doesn't like to close down options and can continue planning or even beginning a draft of a paper without a clear sense of direction. A tutor who prefers judging might be reluctant to let such a student continue on because judging types find closure important. Here, as tutors we need to recognize the strengths of each of these preferences and to encourage students to temper the possible weaknesses of each preference. The perceiving student will work hard to continue finding material for her paper and to write and write in a number of directions, but she needs to learn that she will have to rein in that impulse eventually and get down to some tightening and focus. The tutor who senses this direction in the student's planning might want to give her some time to continue the play of ideas, but should also try to set a deadline. The tutor can both acknowledge the student's strengths and then help to set some limits: "Can you come back with your draft on Thursday so that we can start to talk about your thesis and how you will be organizing your paragraphs?"

By contrast, a judging type is much more likely to plan his outline before he has done enough exploring of his topic. Again, we can acknowledge the strengths of this preference but also help the writer to recognize that structure which is imposed too quickly can cut out useful exploration, planning, and development of ideas. For the student who has been told (too often) to begin with an outline and who is too comfortable with that approach to permit adequate exploration of his topic, it is important for the tutor to realize that this writer may suddenly show great improvement in his writing when he is encouraged to talk, to explore, to float some ideas around in his head before ever taking a pencil in hand to begin that outline. Tutors can recognize symptoms of writers who want very early closure by the writer's actions. Such writers might keep verbally testing out their outlines in the tutorial and asking the tutor if the plan seems acceptable. That is, the tutor needs to watch for the writer who becomes too fixated on getting the outline right. On the other hand, here it is helpful to remind tutors who prefer outlining before they write—usually judging types—that they are prone to feeling very comfortable with a student who is also a judging type. Such tutors are just as likely to be impatient with a student who prefers perceiving. Tutors can suggest outlines, when it seems appropriate, but they have to be ready to accept a writer's preference for "thinking about it for awhile yet."

Deciding on the Tutorial Agenda

When a tutor and student work together, writing center theorists describe the relationship as collaborative. In a truly collaborative setting, this means that when deciding on how to spend their time together, the tutor and the student need to negotiate what their agenda will be. That is, they should come to a mutual decision as to what they hope to accomplish together. This process is usually referred to as "setting the agenda." Early in the tutorial this comes up when the tutor asks, "What do you want to work on today?" The student may or may not have something specific in mind, and the tutor can ask some questions, look at the paper, and offer suggestions as to the goal for the tutorial. But it is not a unilateral decision. During the time that the tutorial conversation is focused on this matter of setting the agenda, it is good for tutors to realize that their personality preferences may play a role here. Some people are not comfortable with making decisions until they are sure that a consensus has been reached; others are more willing to make decisions on their own and let others follow them. Feeling types tend to prefer harmony, and a tutor who prefers feeling over thinking is likely to keep the agenda-setting conversation going longer in order to assure herself that she, her student, and the student's absent teacher will all be comfortable with whatever topic is decided upon. Or, if she is a perceiving type, she may be more inclined to plunge into some tutorial talk before having a clear idea of where they are headed. If she is working with a student who is also a perceiving type, they may enjoy the spontaneous flow of conversation as it carries them forward.

On the other hand, when the student is a judging type, the student can exhibit some uneasiness about what is going on unless there are some indications of how the tutorial is going to take shape. A judging type may want to know how long the tutorial will be, what to expect, or even what the determined topic of the tutorial is. Such a student may sound to the tutor as if she is suspicious about the whole tutoring process because of such questions—perhaps even convey a sense of not wanting to be there. But if we acknowledge that student's need for structure, we will quickly realize that we are actually putting the student at ease by answering as many of the questions as we can before plunging in. Similarly, for a tutor, knowing one's personality preference leads to a clearer picture of how she prefers to proceed in a tutorial. When asked to write about the value of the MBTI to herself and her tutoring, Kristi offered the following:

> I scored high on the [judging] dimension. I am a very organized person, not only in writing, but in other areas of my life. I am not one to do spontaneous

things; I like to know what I am going to be doing and when I am going to be doing it. When it comes to writing, I usually plan everything out and have some direction when I start writing (an outline or a thesis statement). When tutoring, I can see that I feel more comfortable if I have some idea where I am going with the session and where the student is going with his or her paper.

Plunging In

When the tutor and student start reading the student's paper, they may both be sensing types and prefer to begin with details before moving to larger concerns such as what the paper is about. Some sensing tutors have described to me their preference for having to read the whole paper, sentence by sentence, before they are ready to talk with the student. Some students are quite content beginning in that way; others seem resigned to it, assuming (mistakenly) that the tutor is in control. If the student prefers working with information as an intuitive does, then he may also show signs of impatience with questions about details. Other tutors who prefer intuition need to begin by asking what the paper is about and what the assignment is. Tutors and students who are both intuitives are likely to remain more involved with this big picture, and such a tutor should remind herself that they will both have to prod themselves a bit to get back to the details eventually. As with all the MBTI types, we recognize and work with our strengths just as we acknowledge our weaknesses and realize the need to compensate for them. Jeff, a student in one of my tutor training classes, applied this to his own tutoring:

> One of my highest scoring categories was [intuition]. In tutoring, I can help a student develop an overall picture for the paper, but I may have trouble dealing with minute details, one of the more common problems found in papers. Hopefully recognizing this weak area can help me to actively watch for it, and I could relate to students who have similar problems. Then together we could deal with this aspect and come up with ways to improve that area of our writing.

When, as often happens in writing tutorials, tutor and student are working on a paper which takes a stance and defends it, the personality preferences of the two people engaged in the collaboration can affect how the paper is read and valued. For example, I recently observed pairs of tutors-to-be in our training class talking about a student paper on the effects of divorce. As I watched, I noticed one pair of tutors-to-be whose conversation seemed to focus on written evidence of the student's feelings about the divorce. The pair of tutor trainees also talked about how to strengthen the paper's discussion of how the divorce affected the family. They wondered if the writer should have added more details about the writer's unhappiness and loneliness during the divorce. As I walked around the room listening to other pairs of tutors-to-be doing their own analysis of the same paper, I heard very different discussions. One tutor-to-be argued strongly with his partner that some objective principles needed to be applied to the discussion of the effects of divorce. He wondered whether some statistics wouldn't strengthen the point being made by the writer. When the whole class came together, we talked about divergent ways in which arguments can be supported, but we also talked about personal preferences for how to build a strong case for something. Such a discussion must acknowledge that feeling types put heavier stress on human values while thinking types want to apply logic and principles.

Feeling types as tutors should also recognize that they are more likely to be comfortable asking the writer such recommended opening questions as how she felt about her paper or what she liked most or least. These questions can be excellent indicators for what the writer wants to revise, especially when students come to tutorials unsure about what to do next with a draft-in-progress. Thinking types, on the other hand, are more comfortable with objective criteria such as appropriate use of transitions, clear topic sentences, adequate conclusions, grammatical correctness, and so on, and they want to measure a paper's needs against such criteria. And all tutors need to take into account the writer's preferences as well, for while tutors are collaborators, their ultimate responsibility is to help the writer achieve what he or she wants the paper to be, not what the tutor prefers.

Conclusion

There are a number of benefits we derive from all the awareness that type theory gives us. Tutors-to-be move from generic pictures of "the student" with whom they will be working to a more differentiated one of some of the kinds of difference that are possible. They have a better appreciation of the power of the tutorial to work with individual differences and all that the tutorial can accomplish because it permits us to work with each writer in ways that are appropriate for that writer. They begin to define for themselves their own strengths and weaknesses as tutors and as writers and to think about how to compensate for possible weaknesses. They also increase their awareness of what difference really means to them as people. Candice Johnson and Linda Houston, who use the MBTI in their tutor training courses, explain this very well:

> This look into human behavior provides students with a framework for realizing that different does not mean bad. These students learn to see differences as positive; they learn to celebrate the uniqueness of individuals. They come to appreciate that we, as individual members of a society, provide balance for each other. This self-understanding has proven to be a vital link in our tutors' effectiveness. (4)

Finally, there is also some relief that tutors-to-be begin to acknowledge as part of their newly enlarged sense of human differences. Most new tutors begin with assumptions that there are "perfect" or "right" ways to proceed. They want to know what they should do in any given situation, thereby revealing an unspoken assumption that there is only one right way to handle a tutorial and that if they don't know what it is, they will "mess up" the student and the student's paper. Acknowledging and working with human difference permits us to put aside such notions, to free ourselves for the unexpected, and to permit ourselves the luxury of responding with flexibility and insight gained at the moment. Knowing about difference can be very liberating knowledge.

8   Writers, Computers, and Personality

Ronald A. Sudol

Perhaps nothing accentuates personality difference more than change, particularly at a time when change propels the whole of literate society toward communicating digitally. No more pencils. No more books. Words without paper. Lines giving way to networks. Texts vulnerable to radical manipulation. Discourses that motivate and persuade with images and icons. The degree to which these adaptations to electronic communication are stressful or exciting, numbing or inspiring, is, in part, a measure of personality difference.

Two points are worth bearing in mind when we try to understand the personality dimensions of technological change in writing and reading. First, we should remember that the current transition is from one technology to another, not from a stable and normative present to an unstable and abnormal future. Writing with pencils, pens, and typewriters and reading words that have been physically imprinted on paper are processes shaped by the technologies of manuscript and print inscription. The two thousand year history of those technologies established the authority of the word, the book, and the author. Our political, legal, and educational systems—indeed the world as we know it—are products of those technologies. But now changes are afoot. The electronic technologies of communication that began with telephone and television and now include computers and the information super highway have already destabilized the authority of the word and the relevance of the book. Although it is certainly unsettling to imagine a library not as a building full of books but a central computer from which electronically stored information can be retrieved (and changed!), we should resist the notion that this is anything but a shift from one technology to another, bringing with it not the end of the world — or even the word — but a restructuring of the ways we communicate and get things done. The study of personality type helps us understand the value of seeing *different* ways of getting something done, rather than the right way and the wrong way. The new technology is a *different* way of communicating.

The second point worth keeping in mind as we see a new communications technology gradually overtake an older one is that both personality preference and technology are forms of mediation. Each is instrumental in connecting self and other. There is a symbiotic relationship between the array of tools provided by a technology and the array of personality preferences an individual brings to bear on the use of those tools. Change the tools, and the habitual preferences are thrown into disarray. Marshall McLuhan's observation that new technologies extend some senses and amputate others might be modified to apply to preferences. As the tools change, we can expect to see a different pattern in the strengths and weaknesses associated with the various personality types. To take a broad example: the solitude of individual authorship and the privacy of reading that are hallmarks of the world created by print technology is comfortable for the introverted orientation to the world. Electronic communication, on the other hand, with its collaborative networks and malleable texts, may provide more comfort to the extraverted orientation. In any case, the way we write and communicate will be mediated by how our preferences interact with the array of instruments offered by the technology. These are the interactions I would like to explore in the following sections.

How Writers Use Computers

For most of us, word processing has been the gateway to the new technology. Although word processing is clearly an application of digital communications technology, its user interfaces and nomenclature replicate elements of print technology: documents, files, desktop, cut-and-paste, return, page, and — of course — printing. Word processing is thus transitional and provides a good place to observe how personality preferences interact with the tools of the technology.

A provocative essay published in 1990 by Marcia Peoples Halio of the University of Delaware compared the writing of students using either IBM or Macintosh computers ("Student Writing"). Halio found distinct differences in the writing produced by the two groups of students. In the world of computers, anything that happened as long ago as 1990 must be viewed as a quaint antiquity. In those ancient days the IBM operating system was character-based and had the look and feel of print technology transferred to video display. The Macintosh, with its icons and game-like desktop display, was more hip. The work students composed on Macs, Halio found, was sloppy, ungrammatical, slangy, and immature. Moreover, for their subject matter the Mac students seemed drawn to pop culture trivialities. The IBM students, in contrast, were neater, more mature and correct, and chose as their topics enduring issues that could be argued in classical form.

These findings unleashed a frenzy of outraged commentary. Macintosh users flamed their displeasure across e-mail networks, an article in a popular computer magazine wondered "Does the Mac Make You Stupid?" (Levy), and the debate boiled over into formal academic disputation (Youra; Kaplan and Moulthrop; Halio "Maiming Reviewed"). Now that the IBM and the Mac are almost betrothed and starting to look like each other, the quibbles about research methodology, competing pedagogies, and different features of operating systems and applications have little relevance. The differences between the IBM and the Mac were distractions from the main point. Students using IBMs could more easily import into the IBM environment the habits and preferences they had developed using print technology (and the same was probably true of their teachers as well). But the Macintosh of 1990 propelled its users further into the future, wrenching them away from the habits and preferences print technology had shaped. The defects Halio recognized in the writing of her Mac students are the same ones critics quite reasonably even now attribute to the new technology itself. So except for being distracted by the IBM/Macintosh differences, Halio was on the right track in recognizing and recording what was happening to her students.

The system of bipolar personality preferences based on Jungian models provides one way of looking at how student writers make the transition to electronic writing. The computerized writing process is mediated not only by the fluid electronic text environment but also by the way the writer's preferences as to focusing, perceiving, judging, and acting are energized within that environment. In order to take a closer look at how students of various personality types write with a computer, I have, over the past few years, been collecting samples of written testimony from students about their adaptation. Studying these comments in the context of their Myers-Briggs personality types yields some preliminary insights into the range of variation that may be expected when a typical cohort of students makes the transition to electronic writing.

The students were enrolled in typical freshman composition courses in which they were expected to produce the required written work with word processing using computers in university labs or in their own residences. The classroom itself was not computerized, but technical assistance was available in computer labs. Students completed the MBTI early in the semester, and at the end they submitted written responses to specific prompts about how they used the computers.

The prompts were adapted from Jensen and DiTiberio's table of "Writers' Strengths and Weaknesses" (98–99), which contains the condensed essence of their hypotheses about the kinds of performance that may be expected in each of the eight MBTI personality preferences. In their summation of the semester's work the students were asked to respond "yes" or "no" to each of the prompts and to comment on how their use of a computer may have affected their performance in that area. Throughout the semester and again just prior to submitting their summations, the students were coached on the importance of coming to terms with their own assessment of strengths and weaknesses and that a different combination of strengths and weaknesses characterizes writers at every level of competence.

1 I write best when I write about personal experience. [E]
2 My writing is too conversational for academic papers. [E]
3 I am good at condensing ideas in formal papers. [I]
4 My writing seems too formal, and I am reluctant to express feelings and ideas. [I]
5 I am best when I write factual reports. [S]
6 I have trouble showing my reader the ideas behind the facts. [S]
7 I like to take imaginative and original approaches to topics and assignments. [N]
8 My writing is too abstract and flighty and often unsupported by examples and background. [N]
9 I write logically and objectively and excel in organization. [T]

10 My writing is highly structured but lacks personal appeal to the audience. [T]

11 I am good at using personal experience to express my beliefs and personality. [F]

12 My writing is gushy, sentimental, uncritical, and flows without organization. [F]

13 I choose topics easily, write quickly, and have little trouble meeting deadlines. [J]

14 Under the pressure of deadlines my writing can be arbitrary, opinionated, and underdeveloped. [J]

15 I write thoroughly, and my ideas are well developed and supported. [P]

16 My writing can be too broad, often long and tedious, and rambles without conclusion. [P]

The bracketed letters (not included on the original questionnaire) identify each statement as a strength or weakness associated with the eight personality preferences. Whether students answered "yes" or "no" was irrelevant. The purpose was to get them to use their own sense of strengths and weaknesses as a way of commenting on the effects word processing may have had on their writing. The chief reason for designing the inventory according to Jensen and DiTiberio's hypotheses is that the statements range equally across all of the identifiable personality preferences. In keeping with the wellness spirit of the MBTI, the weaknesses are linked with corresponding strengths, the strengths being the odd numbered items and the weaknesses even numbered. Moreover, the inventory itself leaves the MBTI apparatus invisible even while it provides a means for comprehensive self-assessment. This project included no quantifiable features whatsoever. The MBTI reported results and the corresponding questionnaire were used to impose order on the hundreds of responses from these students, most of whom were relatively new to the idea of using word processing for all of their writing.

Extraversion and Introversion

The extraverts and the introverts in the word processing classes responded to the inventory predictably. The extraverts comment at length on the apparent oral and conversational quality of electronic writing, observing the easy, rambling flow of thoughts, the inducement to informality, the flexibility of text generating and editing. They more often than not acknowledge a weakness for an inappropriate conversational style but credit the computer with the power to assist them in editing it into academic respectability. Remarkably, several of them mention that they talk to the computer as if it were another person, the face-like screen and its eye-like display apparently representing an alternative self with whom to engage in dialog. Here are some typical extravert responses from various students:

- Using the word processor . . . is like telling a story to the computer. . . . it is very simple to just keep your thought process going with very few breaks.
- . . . it is so easy to ramble on in a friendly and laid back manner.
- I find that I talk to myself and the computer as if it would answer.
- . . . I am able to use the computer as another person talking to me on the screen.
- . . . helps me express ideas I never knew I had.

So for the extraverts the computer is not just a tool but another opening to the outer world of experience, helping them develop a rhetorical sense of persona and audience.

The introverts have much less to say about the computer's role in encouraging expressiveness. Their most telling comments come in response to statement number 7, "I like to take imaginative and original approaches to topics and assignments" (especially, but not exclusively, if they are also intuitives). Significantly, the extraverts are uncharacteristically silent on this point, observing, when they say anything at all, that creativity has nothing to do with computers. The introverts see the easy flow of text as transcription rather than discovery:

- The word processor makes it easier to write imaginatively because it comes out flowing without a lot of stopping to think . . . .
- The word processor may help taking a second look, but it is the first draft that is usually the most imaginative.
- The speed of recording all my thoughts is so fast that I often ramble on and on for pages before I realize that I have said very little.
- Often when fellow students are proofing for me they remark on the big words (do they really exist?) or my use of words like "thus" and "hence." My formal writing style and interest in sounding knowledge-

able and professional in academic papers makes for very slow and arduous writing. Word processing doesn't seem to help much in this problem, but it does help me organize all the complex points I want to make and rearrange them until I am satisfied—I am never fully satisfied.

In general, the introverts are less sanguine than the extraverts about the easy input of word processing. The word processor does indeed accelerate the transcription and organization of thoughts they have already formed, but it might just as well lead to distractions.

The introverts are also less enthusiastic about the often-lauded community spirit of computer labs:

> I do my best creative writing late at night in a small, quiet, smoky room where I can let my imagination run free which is more difficult to do in a noisy, bright and clinical feeling computer lab. Where's the inspiration?

That private inner world as a source of energy is rarely acknowledged by advocates of computerized classrooms, who have been more impressed by the achievements of extraverts drawing energy from the community spirit of labs and networks. The practical and pedagogical benefits of computerized collaboration are unimpeachable as long as collaboration is not valorized to the extent of short-circuiting the introvert's gift for formulation.

Clearly, neither a single theory of the writing process nor a single set of directives on how best to use word processing is going to be universally helpful. The text entry part of the technology favors the extravert's gift for expressiveness, but in doing so it also exacerbates the extravert's tendency toward superficiality. Accordingly, the focus of instruction for the extraverts could be on nurturing compensatory skills such as forming and editing that employ other features of the technology like multiple windows. For the extravert, software that interrupts the flow of language and diverts it toward depth, development, or deletion provides compensatory nurturing.

While word processing opens a new portal to the extravert's orality, it throws the introvert into deeper privacy where language emerges as a projection of thought already formed. The introverts do not need instruction or even encouragement to ponder and edit, but they do need help in developing the sense of "other" that is fundamental in communication and natural to the extravert. Perhaps recording personal comments in a subtext format would help bring the personal and interactive spirit into the introvert's enterprise. And collaboration can be helpful provided it is aimed at developing the introvert's sense of rhetorical transaction and not displacing the introvert's preferred method of concept formation.

Sensing and Intuition

The differences between sensing and intuitive students is easiest to see when they exhibit their respective weaknesses in writing analytical papers. In an essay of rhetorical or literary criticism, sensing students are the ones who bind themselves to the text with ample illustrations and detailed summary but without showing what is being illustrated or what it all means, and intuitive students take flight from the text by generalizing provocatively but vaguely with little or no illustrative support. The MBTI has been a nearly infallible predictor of these opposing weaknesses among my students. But the intuitives enjoy an advantage. Their weakness for vague abstraction enjoys some level of academic respectability, in the sense that it at least looks like a step in the right direction. Moreover, in word processing intuitive students can revise easily by simply adding examples to sharpen up the abstractions and frameworks they have already formed. The weakness of the sensing students, on the other hand, looks less like incompleteness and more like incompetence—no ideas, no categories, no connections, no going beyond what is obvious. For them, revising will be an agony without guidelines and models. The broad rhetorical scope of most freshman composition courses will confound sensing students more than such highly prescriptive and information-bound courses as technical writing.

Does the computer help students connect facts and ideas? On the basis of the hundreds of student responses I have gone through, it helps the intuitives somewhat (through additive revising) and the sensing types hardly at all. Because its visual elements are still tied to print, word processing elevates the intuition-friendly academic enterprise to the realm of relative ease, automation, and convenience. Thus, it is easier for intuitives to add substance to the frameworks they have brainstormed into text files. But the sensing types find nothing in word processing to help them digest the data they like to focus on. Perhaps a split screen format could be helpful to students with either preference in some cases. One part of the display could contain the text in progress and the other blank space with prompts such as "What's the point?" for sensing types and "Can you support this?" for intuitives.

Although no student in my surveys mentioned it, there may be some benefit to sensing students in what has been called the "accumulative rhetoric" of word processing (Sudol). Word processing encourages the accumulation of data, and although such accumulations may have a harmful effect if they are lumped uncritically into documents, they also provide the basic material sensing students prefer to have readily at hand as they develop their ideas. Cut-and-paste procedures provide endless opportunities to actually look at how various elements might work together. Heuristic procedures, templates, and prompts that automatically ask questions within word processing programs might help the sensing students massage their accumulations into discursive shape.

If word processing is the last, albeit high-tech, manifestation of the era of print technology (Bolter), then other kinds of applications may offer sensing students better support. Easy access to such extensions of word processing as data bases, libraries of prescribed models, outline programs, and sets of paradigms and templates could provide the material foundation for the sensing student's capacity for adaptive creativity. And the data-rich hypertext environment may offer them a more congenial means of organizing information. One reason hypertextual reading and writing seem strange to us is that these processes favor a set of nurtured skills quite different from those that emerged in the era of print technology. Indeed, hypertext's challenge to the writer's authority over the structure of discourse undermines the intuitive's preference for guiding concepts (though as *consumers* of hypertext, intuitives are likely to thrive on its flexibility and openness). Still, when writing becomes a pathway through a multitextual network, sensing students are well equipped to negotiate link by associative link to become reliable pathmakers. They could also benefit from multimedia applications in which sound and image enrich data. In the electronic communications future, such multimedia and multitextual associations may dislodge hierarchical concepts as the fundamental units of knowledge. Some of the peculiar writing Halio observed in the work of her Macintosh students may have been early signs of this epistemological shift.

Thinking and Feeling

Students who use thinking judgment write essays that are logical, objective, analytical, and consistent, but they may be dogmatic, abrasive, impersonal, overly structured, technical, and dry. Students with feeling judgment excel at connecting with the audience, using personal experience, expressing deep conviction, and writing stylishly, but their writing may be gushy and sentimental, lacking a critical edge, loosely organized, and contradictory (Jensen and DiTiberio 98–99). Thinking types and feeling types responded to the questionnaire on using computers very consistently. Thinking students admire the cut-and-paste feature that enables them to keep things in order, whereas feeling students admire the generative sense of flow in digital input. Some feeling types suggest that the technological nature of the computer assists logical thinking. According to one,

> I am forever moving sentences and paragraphs around. They make sense to me, but I feel my reader may have a hard time understanding what I am trying to say. This is where the word processor is a lifesaver. You can move text so easily. It helped make my papers logical.

Of course, the computer does nothing of the kind. It does not make the writing more logical, but it may help make it more rhetorical. Although the writing already made sense to the writer, this feeling type student characteristically used the computer's fluid text environment to revise for the benefit of the reader. The writer's assumption that the writing became more logical *because of the computer* provides a salutary reminder that logic is a function of point of view and the servant of rhetoric. Most feeling types acknowledge the computer's organizational assistance but deny its influence on how they think. The computer's organizational power, for them, is reader-centered. For the thinking students, on the other hand, it is writer-centered, guiding their own developing thoughts: "Once I am to the point where my organization is able to be followed, then everything I write is logical and direct. The word processor helped by making the organization happen much sooner than it usually does."

The behavior and observations of thinking and feeling students illustrate how they can use computers to nurture compensatory skills. The whole process of taking a writing course, in even the most supportive setting, focuses attention on weaknesses to overcome. Thinking students need to learn to be less dogmatic and topic-oriented and more flexible and personal; feeling students need to learn to be less sentimental and rambling and more critical and clear. Students who are aware of such shortcomings are able quite naturally to use computers in compensatory ways. The thinking students take advantage of the easy flow of text input to bring a greater sense of orality and conversation into their drafts. Although their thinking preference attracts them to cut-and-paste editing, they quickly learn to use it to try out alternative patterns on readers, signaling an important compensatory shift in the way they work. Feeling students seem to be chastened into organizational awareness by the precision of the whole technological environment. The computer allows them to propose organizational patterns flexibly enough so that their natural preference for allowing the language to flow is not subverted. Still, from what I have seen, thinking students get the better deal with computers. It is easier for them to use computers to loosen up their writing than it is for feeling students to tighten up theirs.

Judging and Perceiving

The writing processes of judging and perceiving writers are easy to observe. Judging writers find a thesis, develop a plan, follow the plan expediently, and dispose of the task quickly with more editing (for closure) than revising (for expansion). They will probably not change their thesis or plan along the way unless they have developed compensatory perception skills. Perceiving writers delay closure and gather more information while searching for an elusive thesis. They write long papers, extensively revised, highly inclusive, though they may proceed aimlessly unless they have developed compensatory judging skills (Jensen and DiTiberio 67–71).

Teachers and textbooks are full of advice on how students should go about getting things written. Unfortunately, this advice usually projects one preference and its corresponding process as normative. You either find a thesis, make a plan, and execute it, or you begin writing in order to discover or construct your ideas along the way. Neither species of advice, if adopted exclusively, allows much room for adjusting process to personality. Of course, experienced teachers encourage students to find a process that works best for them, but under the pressure of trying to write well enough to avoid embarrassment, students are more likely to seek a methodological solution to the problem of writing and thus may embrace a single recommended process inappropriately. The population of students, teachers, and other people is split on the JP index and will remain that way through all the pendulum swings and paradigm shifts of the academic enterprise. So we should be cautious about prescribing processes without reference to the range of individual personality differences.

Word processing enables judging writers to execute their preferred processes with greater efficiency than print technologies. They create text around outlines they have already plotted out in a text file. Conclusions can be written first. As one judging student points out: "I begin writing my conclusion in the middle of a file. I like to have my conclusion written beforehand so that all my arguments lead up to it and my paper has direction." Word processing manuals and tutorials seem to have been written by and for judging types, their directives for entering and editing text assuming the writer is already fully informed about the subject matter and wants to express it as quickly as possible. One potential trap here is excessive editing. As another judging student writes: "I tend to edit, re-edit, and re-re-edit endlessly what may have been a perfectly good paper to begin with." In the domain of writing, the judging type's critical acuity is easily turned against his or her own prose, a process encouraged by easy text editing ("The computer is helpful in letting me go back and weed out all the junk that shouldn't be there."). The impetus for such rigorous attention is that closure seems just one or two ruthless keystrokes away. In addition, the finished appearance of word processed text, even in electronic display, supports the judging type's rush to closure. Nevertheless, word processing provides an excellent environment in which the judging student can develop compensatory perceptive skills because it weakens the tyranny of an existing draft. Trying out alternatives in a flexible text environment and viewing electronic text as provisional can easily be accommodated by the framework of the judging type's preferred process.

Perceiving students feel liberated by the computer, and their expansive rambles seem validated by a technology that encourages the accumulation of text and data. But there are trade-offs, as one perceiving student observes, perhaps revealing more than intended:

> Using word processing can make it easy to write an entire paper without really thinking about what you say. Before the word processor I had to think out every sentence before I wrote it so it usually came out pretty near its final form. However, it takes longer to write something that way and with deadline pressure the word processor can be a good way to get a quick start and then go from there.

The student seems to be admitting that the slower mechanical process forced her to think—reflecting, perhaps, years of judging type instruction. Indeed, even perceiving students are much less likely to view freewriting in a text file as a form of thinking. Instead, they appreciate, as this student does, the way the computer helps them generate text. When a perceiving type develops some judging skills, however, the result can be impressive:

It is easy to write too much when using the word processor, but it is also easy to condense things after you have a draft. So in one way it can be a problem because it is easy to ramble without being forced to get to the point, yet it isn't a huge problem because revising and editing are also very easy to do.

Still, apart from the technical ease of editing, there is nothing in the computer to help the perceiving type sharpen rhetorical judgment. That must still come from outside. So the computer encourages perceiving students to use their preference for tentative gathering but offers relatively little assistance in nurturing compensatory judging skills. In contrast, the computer offers relatively little help to judging students' preference for order, but it does help them develop the compensatory perceiving skills of expanding and considering alternatives.

Implications for the Classroom

Computer software, operating systems, and interfaces are human inventions reflecting the personalities of their makers and their interpretations of how people perform tasks. Added to the new grammars of technology itself these all-encompassing systems and networks have become a brave new world to those whose habits of mind and heart have been formed in an era of print literacy. In calling upon teachers to be technology critics by keeping abreast of technological change, Cynthia Selfe makes these useful observations:

> [Teachers] must force themselves to adopt the habit of systematically observing students working with technology in ways that seem unusual, of making notes about these observations, and of looking for patterns within these observations. They must seek out those places and times when students' learning with technology seems to resist traditional educational patterns. Teachers in virtual environments must, in other words, get used to being unsure of what they know and realize that this feeling of dissonance can be productive in leading to new knowledge. (29)

To this sound advice I would add that the Myers-Briggs framework of personality preferences provides the kind of system that would keep such observations of technological adaptation firmly grounded in common knowledge about human functioning.

The chart below outlines some of my own observations, which are limited to preferences (E, F, P, etc.) rather than types (ESFP, etc.) and represent a snapshot of students having widely varied levels of experience and using a rapidly developing technology. In any group of students we can expect to find a full range of personality preferences, so there can be no single set of directives to guide classroom practice beyond emphasizing the value of understanding the full range of variation. Clearly, the way we teach writing will need to change along with the technology, and our best guide may be observations such as these, which attempt to connect student performance with specific features of the technology. For each of the eight personality preferences I have identified such items as either "Natural" or "Compensatory." These categories correspond roughly with the strengths (natural) and weaknesses (compensatory) usually associated with the preferences. The items labeled "Natural" identify areas where the technology magnifies strengths, and the items labeled "Compensatory" identify activities that might help overcome the ways in which the technology might magnify weaknesses for some personality preferences. Certainly instruction should allow for all possible strengths to be magnified, but the focus of most instruction is inevitably centered on helping students devise compensatory strategies.

Extravert

Natural:
- easy flow of language in electronic text environment
- use of video display as other self
- another opening to the outer world
- computer labs and networks as another source of energy

Compensatory:
- adjust for oral, conversational, informal flow of language where inappropriate
- look for program features that encourage critical questioning and forming of easy input

Introvert

Natural:
- text processing speeds up the transcription and organization of ideas

Compensatory:
- use networking to tap the energy of others without losing the privacy of the individual writing space
- delay self-critical revision

Sensing

Natural:
- information-rich computer environment aids data accumulation
- malleable text environment allows data manipulation
- cut-and-paste allows visual tryouts of how facts and ideas could be connected

Compensatory:
- try automated heuristics, outlines, templates, models
- use hypertext and multimedia to aid invention
- try split screen to open space for self-reflexive comments on making sense of information

Intuitive

Natural:
- excellent opportunities for brainstorming, freewriting, and other modes of creative thinking outside of document files

Compensatory:
- become comfortable with information-rich environment and recognize the rhetorical power of information
- try split screen to open space for self-reflexive comments on using information to support ideas

Thinking

Natural:
- the logic of computing supports the logic of discourse
- text environment allows the structure of thought to be displayed and developed

Compensatory:
- allow the easy flow of language to give human voice to discourse

Feeling

Natural:
- easy input outside of document files provides an outlet for feelings and a forum in which to display and examine them

Compensatory:
- don't let technological basis of computing create a false sense of logical coherence

Judging

Natural: ▪ easy to shape a discourse to an existing plan

Compensatory: ▪ distinguish between formative revising and final editing
▪ resist premature closure fostered by elegant on-screen document formats
▪ accept the provisional character of a text-in-progress

Perceiving

Natural: ▪ computer environment opens vast new worlds to exploration

Compensatory: ▪ use a separate text file to develop a sense of audience and to come to terms with other rhetorical constraints
▪ distinguish between generating *text* and generating *meaning*

Considering all of this material together, my hunch—and it is *only* a hunch—is that the technology offers the greatest opportunities for magnifying strengths to extraverts and sensing types. At the same time, it offers the greatest developmental challenge to feeling types and perceiving types. Of course, overcoming a high challenge can lead to high achievement.

These complex interactions between personality preferences and digital technology present particular challenges to us as teachers. Our students' personality variations already confound any of our efforts to be singular and directive when our methodologies seem to favor some gifts rather than others. Add digital technology to the classroom, and the need for non-directive teaching in a pluralistic setting increases. Ironically, teaching with the new technology should help revive the Western world's oldest bag of teaching tricks—rhetoric. From the standpoint of personality type theory, we might define rhetoric as "the art of managing difference." Communication is complex and problematic precisely because we—individuals, groups, societies—are cut off on all sides by chasms of difference. Learning how to create meaning across those chasms has been the focus of rhetorical instruction since the Greeks and Romans invented the curriculum we still use—fitting the discourse to the situation, knowing your audience, understanding yourself, practicing a variety of modes and aims, inventing, rehearsing, polishing.

In claiming that rhetoric provides the key to teaching with types in the new technology, I follow the lead of Richard A. Lanham in his book *The Electronic Word: Democracy, Technology, and the Arts.* Lanham argues that digital writing enhances human intelligence by allowing the manipulation of words and images to undermine the authority of texts. The personal computer radically enfranchises the perceiver, calls attention to the ornamental surface of language, and promotes a new self-consciousness about the playful dynamics of words. Digital writing helps us look *at* words as well as *through* them. Language will be not merely a transparent medium to communicate the eternal truth, as it has been in the era of manuscript and print technology. It also dramatizes the process of adapting to different discourse communities and situations through a self-conscious performative game. Digital technology gives more emphasis to form, style, and strategy—and teaching these features of rhetoric should no longer be neglected, according to Lanham's argument. The bi-polar dynamics of personality difference fit this new-old pedagogy well. Applying the unique patterns of natural and compensatory gifts to the transactions between self and other is a decidedly rhetorical performance, and one that is likely to be magnified by the protean and interactive qualities of electronic writing.

Works Cited

Bolter, Jay David. *Writing Space: The Computer, Hypertext, and the History of Writing.* Hillsdale, NJ: Lawrence Erlbaum, 1991.

Halio, Marsha Peoples. "Maiming Re-Viewed." *Computers and Composition* 7.3 (August 1990): 103–107.

——. "Student Writing: Can the Machine Maim the Message?" *Academic Computing* 4 (January 1990): 16–19.

Jensen, George H. and John K. DiTiberio. *Personality and the Teaching of Composition.* Norwood, NJ: Ablex, 1989.

Kaplan, Nancy, and Stuart Moulthrop. "Other Ways of Seeing." *Computers and Composition* 7.3 (August 1990): 89–102.

Lanham, Richard A. *The Electronic Word: Democracy, Technology, and the Arts.* Chicago: U of Chicago P, 1993.

Levy, Steven. "Does the Mac Make You Stupid?" *Macworld* (November 1990): 69–78.

McLuhan, Marshall. *Understanding Media: The Extensions of Man.* New York: MacGraw, 1964.

Selfe, Cynthia. "Preparing English Teachers for the Virtual Age: The Case for Technology Critics." *Re-Imagining Computers and Composition: Teaching and Research in the Virtual Age.* Ed. Gail E. Hawisher and Paul LeBlanc. Portsmouth, NH: Boynton/Cook, 1992.

Sudol, Ronald A. "The Accumulative Rhetoric of Word Processing." *College English* 53 (December 1991). 920–932.

Youra, Steven. "Computers and Student Writing: Maiming the Macintosh (A Response)." *Computers and Composition* 7.3 (August 1990): 81–88.

9 Picturing the Writing Process: Personality Clues to a Pedagogy of Library Research

Vicki Tolar Collins

As libraries are transformed from orderly buildings filled with books to state-of-the-art stops on the information superhighway, many inexperienced student writers are struggling to make the transition from a Dewey-Decimal, card-catalog world to the intimidating universe of information technology, mystifying menus, and bookless searches, often with only a library map, "search strategy" handout, and tape tour to guide them.

And while many college writing programs have eliminated assignments requiring library research, arguing that such research is discipline-specific and should be taught in the student's major department, faculty across the curriculum are vigorously protesting that they are neither prepared nor willing to teach library research strategies, documentation formats, and skills such as smooth incorporation of borrowed information. "Students should already know those things," they maintain. So inexperienced writers are largely alone in their struggles with documented library papers.

I believe this constitutes a case of neglect across the curriculum. If, as teachers of writing, we are sincere in our professed interest in the whole writing process, we must identify and attend to the needs of these students. This article will explore the varied processes of inexperienced writers in the library through personality type and suggest how awareness of type can help teachers and librarians respond to student need.

Situating the Research

All inexperienced writers in the library are not alike. Their writing processes and affective responses to library research writing may vary as much from student to student as they do from student to professor. My work with college freshmen doing library research suggests that students' attitudes toward the library experience, their success or frustration with accessing the library's systems, and their approach to using sources in their writing may be, at least in part, a function of personality type.

The study on which this article is based involves a class of freshmen who had just completed their first documented library paper, an argument requiring at least three library sources. Before beginning their own research project, these students had taken a tape tour of the library, had received one hour of library instruction from the head reference librarian, and had completed a hands-on search exercise. The college counseling center had administered the Myers-Briggs Type Indicator to this class as a part of my research on composition and personality type.

When my students submit an essay, I usually ask them to write a process memo in class on the due date, a sort of metacognitive reflection on their own writing process on the assignment. Typical questions are: What do you like about your essay? What problems did you have writing it, and how did you solve them? What aspect of your writing do you want me to focus on in responding to this essay?

This time, however, I asked them to respond visually. Just before they turned their research essays in, I said, "I want you to draw a picture that depicts your writing process on this paper. Your drawing or graphic may take any form, but it should include at least these four things: yourself, your sources, your text (i.e., your essay), and your reader." I then wrote "self," "sources," "text," and "reader" on the board.

My students produced drawings rich with affective and cognitive representations. But what interests me most is that students with the same personality type tended to represent their writing process with similar images. In reading these drawings through type, I chose core functions of personality type as the primary sorting criteria. George Frisbie argues for the use of core functions as an analytical tool in his 1988 article in the *Journal of Psychological Type*, pointing out that Isabel Myers, who designed the type indicator, suggested the usefulness of core functions in personality research. The core function combinations are ST (sensing and thinking), NF (intuitive and feeling), SF (sensing and feeling), and NT (intuitive and thinking). According to Mary McCaulley, these combinations reflect cognitive processes, and behaviors common to each function combination could be called a cognitive style. (Core functions as distinguishing features of cognitive style have been used extensively in studies with scientists, management theory and practice, and teachers and students.)

Though much of cognitive learning theory seeks to de-emphasize the affective domain, Jungian type theory includes feeling as an aspect of cognition. The drawings of my students offer us some intriguing insights into personality type and cognitive process.

STs: Struggling in the Stacks

The first drawings are by the STs, the sensing-thinking students. Type theory describes them as concerned with detail, orderly and precise, careful about rules and procedures, and interested in facts oriented with logic. As a type, they are good at observing and ordering, filing and recalling, and sequencing and categorizing.

(Fig. 1) In this drawing notice that the sources are represented quite specifically. The student labels the section of the library "Negative aspects of having handicapped children" and notes "35 million more books on this topic in next aisle, too." The writer is portrayed as distressed—she is crying because she doesn't agree with the facts. Being an ST, she usually trusts the facts, the data, so this puts her in a quandary. Of the four things she was asked to represent, please notice that we see the writer, the sources, and the text, but no reader (unless we are to assume the writer at the podium is her own reader).

(Fig. 2) In the second ST drawing the sources are again represented specifically: *Reader's Guide* is labeled. Again the student is dissatisfied with the sources, which he labels "All BS." Notice that his hair is standing on end. What settled his hair down was a typical ST solution: he found the right machine to use. Now everything is fine, and he is able to produce his text. Again, we have an ST representing the writer, his sources, his text, but no reader, even though that was part of the assignment.

(Fig. 3) The next ST also has hair standing on end. The sources are specific, although shown to be too complicated and written in Russian. When representing his text, he shows, in typical ST fashion, the organization of the paper. In this drawing, the reader does appear vaguely, as a

Figure 1   ISTJ

Figure 2   ## eSTp

Sun & Mon & Tues

Late Tues.

Tues.

1:00 A.M.

Figure 3

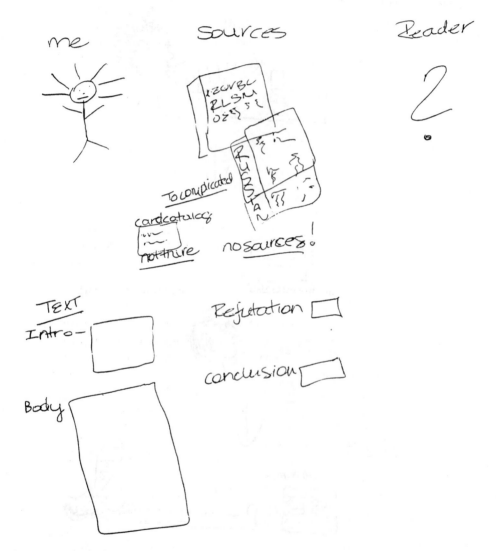

word over to the side with a question mark under it, as if to ask "What is a reader?" or "What does the reader have to do with anything?"

(Fig. 4) The last ST drawing is reminiscent of the first because the writer shows himself faced with two roads: one, the sunny road, is paved with his information; the other, a stormy route, is paved with his stand on the issue. His head is spinning. Somewhere vaguely in the middle are his text and the reader.

What we might learn about the research process of sensing-thinking students from these drawings is that they are able to gather data and access the machinery of doing research. Because they are used to trusting the facts, they are distressed when the facts do not match their preconceived notions on the topic. The affective representations of the STs indicate tears, fear (hair standing on end), and confusion (head spinning). Finally, the reader appears to play virtually no part in the composing process of these sensing-thinking students.

When sensing-thinking students undertake library research, they may need teacher support in three main areas:

1 understanding that personal beliefs and informed opinions are not necessarily the same thing;
2 learning to select sources from among the many items available; and
3 becoming more aware, during the composing process, of the reader's concerns.

Responding to ST students means understanding that when the facts in sources do not match students' preconceived notions on a topic, they may have difficulty identifying a position on their topic which is both authentic for the writer and supportable by research. A teacher might support ST writers in overcoming this dilemma by introducing the notion that previously held beliefs and informed positions may not be identical. People sometimes adhere to beliefs based on assumptions which are contrary to fact or based on tradition or over-generalization. Having students analyze together the assumptions behind some such beliefs may make them more aware of their own tendency in this direction.

An exercise might focus on a series of statements such as "Some people believe women should not be law enforcement officers." This might be based on generalizations such as, "Police officers must be physically powerful," and further on the assumptions, "All police work requires physical strength," and "Women are not strong enough to do police work." The underlying belief that "Police work is too dangerous for women," might

Figure 4　　　　ISTP

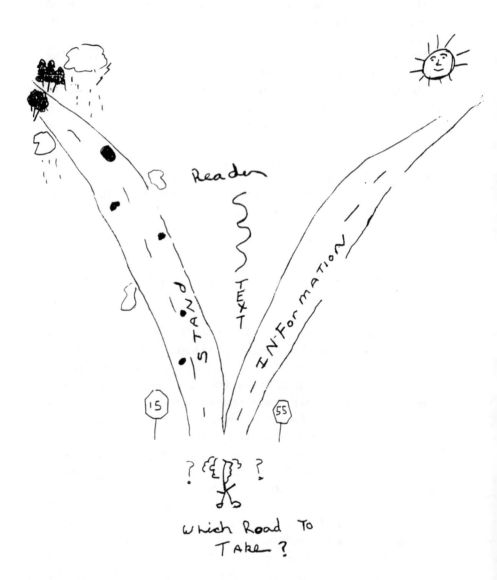

be based on assumptions such as "Women should be protected from danger by men" and "Women are not as courageous as men." After considering statements like these as a class or in small groups, students might be asked to analyze their own attitudes, assumptions, and underlying beliefs about their own topic, looking especially for areas that might be based more on tradition or generalization than on evidence.

The second area of struggle for ST students is helping them learn to select the most appropriate sources from among the many items available. This might involve discussion of the importance of:

- date of publication (When is most recent best?)
- background/authority of the author (How do I discover this?)
- scholarly reputation of the source (When is an article in a scholarly journal more valuable than an article in *USA Today*?)
- the context in which the author writes
- type and documentation of evidence used to support the author's position.

This discussion would, of course, be valuable for most students, but often this information is discussed in a classroom lecture before students have concretely confronted the multitude of sources they will have to choose from. Some evaluation of sources *in medias res* would also be helpful.

A third trait which the teacher might address is the tendency of the ST writer to ignore audience. As Peter Elbow suggests in his essay, "Closing My Eyes as I Speak," some writers ignore audience, at least early in the writing process, to protect themselves from either being paralyzed by audience expectations or lured by the temptation to tell the audience what they want to hear. The difficulty STs have arriving at an authentic position on a topic might only be exacerbated by the pressure of audience awareness. However, later in the writing process, when the student has formulated a position and selected supporting data, the teacher can encourage STs to identify the intended audience and what evidence will be persuasive to this audience. In other words, in the case of drawing #4, wait until the student has selected a road and chosen a vehicle before asking him to take the reader along on the journey.

NFs: Leslie with a Lead Pipe in the Library

The next group of drawings are by NFs, the intuitive-feeling students. Type theory describes them as insightful, creative, original, seeing life as a seamless whole, and good at forming hypotheses and making new combinations. These are people who like people. However, the drawings of my NF students reveal a darker side to the type.

(Fig. 5) In this drawing, the sources are not specifically represented, but they are personified. They mock the writer, saying, "Ha Ha! You can't find me and you never will!" The reader is portrayed positively, saying "I'll come help you!" But the writer is stabbing the text, her own essay. This is one of the most interesting aspects of the drawings: most of the NFs depicted violence in their drawings, which seems counter to type because as a group this personality type tends to be helpful and people-oriented. These particular NF students had the non-violent career goals of becoming a missionary, working with deaf children, becoming a graphic designer, and becoming a TV newscaster.

(Fig. 6) In the next drawing the violence depicted is arson of the library, with the writer as both perpetrator and victim crying "Help!" Sources are all general and labeled "No Good." By Wednesday afternoon, however, the writer's hair has calmed back down and she has a finished text. This is the only NF drawing that omits the reader.

(Fig. 7) In the next NF drawing, the victim of the violence is the student himself. The reader and text are represented as horses. His reader is pulling him one way; his text is pulling him another way; and those burdensome sources are a one-million-pound weight tied to his feet. Is this student being drawn and quartered, or is he a Christ figure?

(Fig. 8) The last NF drawing does not contain overt violence, but the writer is isolated behind a brick wall made up of sources. Nevertheless the writer manages to float a balloon of text up over the wall and connect with the reader after all. The reader and writer become partners in making meaning.

These drawings suggest that the intuitive-feeling students are more aware of audience than the sensing-thinking group. However, the system-accessing aspect of library research is difficult for NFs, involving their emotions to the point where they feel either as if they are the victims of violence or as if they could commit violence themselves.

The central problem of NF students, who gather data through intuition and trust their feelings in decision making, is that in the linear, multi-layered systems of the library, data cannot be located through intuition nor search strategies designed through emotion. The tendency of these students to ignore logic and skim over details during a library search may

Figure 5

eNFj

Figure 6

iNFp

Library was set on fire
by three Winthrop students
late last nights (Joy, Lisa, + John!)

Figure 7   ıNFᴘ

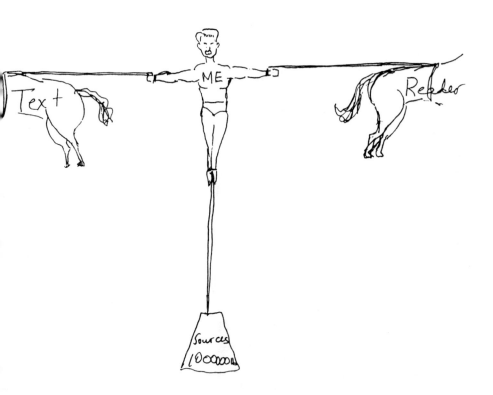

Figure 8　　　　　　ＥNFJ

produce chaos, frustration, and the feeling that suitable sources are forever lost in the dangerous depths of the library. As hours pass and frustrations with the library mount, no wonder the NF students feel drawn to violence.

The good news is that NFs usually respond positively to the care and concern of others. Teachers and librarians can be sensitive to the fact that the NF student may need personal help in accessing the systems and technologies of the library. The more frustrated they are by their failure to find materials, the less able they are to attend to detail, so teachers may want to help these students slow down the search process and master one stage of the system at a time. Teachers might also schedule library orientation and require a general library seek-and-find exercise several weeks before students begin individual searches. Students might even search in teams, since NF students tend to value personal interaction and might experience less stress in a group. Granted, at some point, every researcher is on her own in the stacks. Nevertheless, every act of support and encouragement along the way can make it easier for the NF student to overcome frustration and develop the ability to think logically and attend to the details and order of a search.

The drawing with the horses and weights pulling the student apart can serve to remind teachers that feeling types can be torn by conflicting demands. Unlike the ST student, the NF is all too aware of the reader's expectations and needs and would like to satisfy them. The logical orientation of the women-as-police exercise described earlier may not satisfy the NF student, who rather needs to trust himself or herself to make sound decisions about research problems. Teachers and librarians can empower NFs with encouraging words and urge them to become active problem-solvers rather than victims of the library. Team assignments with some built-in structure could prove helpful to these students.

SFs: Making Friends With Sources

The next type is the SF—the sensing-feeling student. Type theory describes the SF as fact-oriented, interpersonal, sympathetic and friendly, a nurturer and supporter, and good at empathizing, cooperating, and personalizing. With only one SF in the class, no pattern of response can be offered, but the one SF drawing is interesting as a blend of elements of the previous two types.

(Fig. 9) This drawing shows that the writer began research feeling separated from her sources by a moat of sharks. Danger and the potential for violence clearly exist. But she was able to make friends with her sources—in fact she personifies them and shows herself holding hands with the sources. She also personifies her own text, which is smiling at her. The reader, however, is looking the other way.

While the one SF student in this study seemed particularly well suited for the tasks of the library search, other SFs may find library work isolating unless they are allowed to work in pairs or groups. Because SF students learn well through instruction that includes personal involvement, library instruction that is hands-on will be particularly valuable to these students: tours, sample search exercises, opportunities to experiment with computer and CD-rom searches. These are the students who may be most likely to use a map of library holdings.

NTs: Reader as Jaws

The last group is the NTs, the intuitive thinkers. Type theory describes them as speculative, emphasizing understanding, able to synthesize and interpret, and good at problem solving and comparing and contrasting. The NT's goal is to think things through.

(Fig. 10) In the first NT drawing the sources are represented vaguely and labeled "Book." This writer anticipates that the text will shock the reader because it says that some people don't want to have amniocentesis.

(Fig. 11) The last drawing is the most complex and is also by an NT. This student flatteringly portrays the instructor as a shark who rips the writer's paper apart and trashes it. On the distant horizon we see an island called Spring Break. The student notes "Could have used it to get away from shark, but didn't." Courage in the face of danger. Also on the horizon is the ship USS Rescue—Drop/Add. In this drawing, not only has the evil shark trashed the student's text, she also devoured the writer. Nevertheless he has managed to access the sources, apparently without trouble. But his text is represented as in the fog, unclear, and the path between the text and the reader is blocked by fire.

To interpret the intuitive-thinking drawings, we need to remember that more than any other group, the NT values his or her own competence. This is probably reflected in the stressful depictions of the writer-reader relationship in these drawings. Perhaps because of the thinking prefer-

Figure 9   ıSFᴘ

Figure 10   eNTj

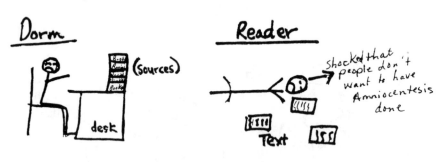

Figure 11   eNTp

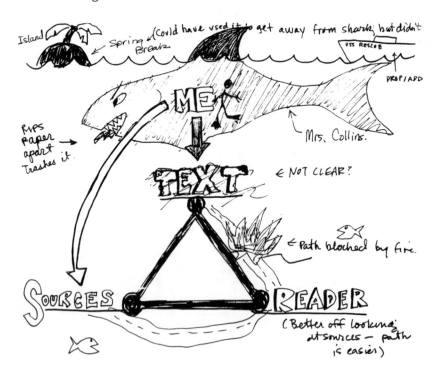

ence, the logic of the library's organization makes sense to the NT, so accessing information does not present a major problem. NTs learn well through organized teacher lectures and so may find librarian-led classroom instruction valuable. Because NTs enjoy self-instruction, they may also learn from computer-designed programs for library training. There remains, however, the NT's anxiety concerning reader response to his or her text.

The NT student seems most to need teacher support in forming realistic expectations of herself in relation to the reader. NTs respond well to frequent positive feedback during the writing process. They might be encouraged to think through audience needs and attitudes using freewriting, paired conversation, or teacher conference in order to increase their own sense of writing competence and to reduce fear of the reader as devouring shark. They will also gain confidence from clearly explained expectations for the assignment and from evaluative teacher responses that affirm rather than "trash" or "burn" the student's text.

Interpreting the Clues: Implications for Teachers

A pedagogy of the research paper which responds to personality type is, finally, the main subject of this essay. This pedagogy will honor individual differences among students, teachers, and librarians in light of varied preferences for gathering data and making decisions; in light of the complex systems of the library; and in light of the myriad choices writers must make in searching and composing. This pedagogy challenges the conventional wisdom of a single "model search strategy," acknowledging that students will experience the search and composing processes in a range of ways. It also affirms the roles of both cognitive and affective domains in library tasks.

This pedagogy invites teachers and librarians to attend to differences among students. And it invites students to stretch beyond their preferred modes of learning and deciding to gain new and necessary competences as searchers and writers. This pedagogy also acknowledges that student research experiences are qualified by many elements in addition to personality type: by gender, race, class, physical capabilities, geographic location, literacy history, and numerous other factors. While no single approach can account for or respond to all problems students experience in library research, personality type is one important factor to consider, one perspective through which teachers can approach and support writers of research papers.

Identifying various sites of student struggle indicates why traditional library lectures and tours, linear search strategies, and task-by-task due dates do not provide adequate instructional framework and support for students to experience success with the library paper. While these traditional training approaches appear to be designed by linear thinkers for linear thinkers, even the most linear students, the STs, need additional instruction and support. These results also indicate the importance of affective support for all students during the project.

What constitutes "affective support" for students? Support can take the form of verbal and written encouragement; demonstrations of patience with student struggles; and expressions of confidence which urge students to stretch, persevere, learn new skills in the library, and try new approaches to composing. Support can also be the careful crafting of whole class, small group, and individual learning experiences which address problem areas of the search process. Awareness of type enables teachers to structure cooperative assignments which draw on strengths of certain students to expand the skills and understanding of their classmates. Table 1 suggests several ways that teachers might recognize and respond to certain types of struggles students experience in the library. One point to note is that no students indicated documentation format or incorporation of sources to be a problem. This may be because students had practiced these skills through small group in-class assignments before beginning work in the library.

The data of this study represents a very small sample of students and clearly cannot be seen as providing conclusive results, but the drawings do offer insights which might help us as we introduce students to the process of doing library research and producing a documented text. Most helpful is the insight we gain into the location of angst and struggle for each core personality type in writing the library paper.

Understanding type can bring benefits to students, teachers, librarians, and scholars in composition. My experience indicates that students who understand type theory and know their own type preferences are better able to work through problematic aspects of writing tasks because they are more sure of their own strengths and more patient with their weaknesses.

But even if individual type data is unknown for a particular group of students, type awareness enables teachers to recognize students' different struggles and provide varied approaches in library instruction and support. Teachers can urge students to develop competence in their less-preferred dimensions when the situation demands it. For example, doing library research requires attention to detail, which is a sensing skill. Intuitive types learn the hard way that if they don't write down the whole call number of the book, they probably won't be able to find it on the shelf. The Library of Congress system does not accommodate global thinkers.

Another point is that teachers and librarians (as well as researchers) have personality preferences, too. Awareness of our own preferences can make us more effective and sensitive in working with student writers. This can be illustrated by returning to the drawing of a student in this study who is much like me in personality type. He is the NT who sees me as a shark. Is this just because he is overly sensitive to audience reaction (as am I)? Or is this because I am, in fact, most critical of the writing of the student who is most like me? Type theory can sensitize us to our own prejudices.

I also believe that by asking students to reflect on their writing processes and communicate those reflections, as my students did in their drawings, we affirm the value of each student's process and we affirm our students as writers. The information they share about their writing processes helps us recall how it feels to be an inexperienced writer working in the complexity of a university library for the first time.

Type considerations open interesting avenues for further research in composition studies. Research is needed to assess the cognitive and affective outcomes for students who receive type-centered support while writing research papers. The increasing use of complex technology in library searches provides another fertile area for type exploration. Several readers of this essay have wondered about the variable of gender with type in library research. These and other areas remain to be explored by believers and doubters of type theory.

In conclusion, I want to affirm that our theories influence what we believe about people and how we interact with them. Type theory supports the notion that although individuals have certain preferences, they can develop along each type dimension. When we use clues of personality type to help students learn the important skills of library research and composing with borrowed information, we can be sensitive to type differences, we can be alert to our students' frustrations and fears, and we can help them develop new strengths that will make them wiser, bolder, and less tortured researchers and writers.

Teaching Strategies for the Library Research Paper
(by Core Function of Personality Type)

Type	Behaviors/Strengths	Learning Preferences
ST	Enjoys detail	Demonstrations
	Tuned in to systems	Lab
	May have strong personal views	Television
	Values own position	Having a plan and sticking to it
NF	Is able to see the big picture	Personal relationships
	Values relationships and feelings of others	Dislikes impersonal, didactic instruction
		Values faculty feedback
	May ignore or be oblivious to details and logical structure	Values student enthusiasm
		Enjoys low-friction, student-led discussion
SF	Good with details and systems	Student-led demonstration and presentations
	Values personal interaction	Instruction with personal involvement
		Television
		Films and AV
		Having a study schedule
NT	Logical and organized	Organized teacher lectures
	Intuitive	Self-instruction
	Understands systems	Reading
	Values own competence	Systematically organized (courses) exercises

Note: "Learns Through" column adapted from Jensen and DiTiberio, *Personality and the Teaching of Composition*. Ablex, 1989.

Library/Research Stress Points	Teaching Strategies
May be overwhelmed by finding too much data	Teach students to evaluate and prioritize sources
May experience conflict between preconceived notions and new data	Present exercises on uncovering hidden assumptions
May ignore audience	Allow students to postpone consideration of audience until late in writing process
May not comprehend or enjoy complex, impersonal library systems	Through small group exercises, allow practice of accessing the system
May find solitary library work isolating	Allow the option of collaborative research projects
Ignoring details may make accessing library systems frustrating	Frequently remind NFs of the importance of tracking sources through specific detail
May feel pressure to accommodate all readers	Design small group exercises in audience analysis
May see library paper as "cut and dried"	Provide opportunities to be creative throughout
May resist solitary library work	Provide in person or video library orientation including hands-on experiences
May be intimidated by authority of sources	Allow students to work in pairs and present projects based on their research
	Teach students to evaluate and prioritize sources
May resent difficult searches which put competence in question	Structure assignment so that search competence is rewarded (e.g., NTs might assist NFs in accessing library systems)
May be overly concerned about reader reaction	Make evaluation criteria clear at the outset
	Work on audience analysis
	Use self-evaluation to affirm competence and appropriateness for readers

Appendix 1
Descriptions of the Sixteen Types

by Gordon D. Lawrence, Ph.D.

Words to Help Understanding of Type Concepts

E: EXTRAVERSION
When extraverting, I am...

Oriented to the outer world
Focusing on people and things
Active
Using trial and error with confidence
Scanning the environment for
  stimulation

I: INTROVERSION
When introverting, I am...

Oriented to the inner world
Focusing on ideas, inner impressions
Reflective
Considering deeply before acting
Finding stimulation inwardly

S: SENSING PERCEPTION
When using my sensing, I am...

Perceiving with the five senses
Attending to practical and factual
  details
In touch with the physical realities
Attending to the present moment
Confining attention to what is said
  and done
Seeing "little things" in everyday life
Attending to step-by-step experience
Letting "the eyes tell the mind"

N: INTUITIVE PERCEPTION
When using my intuition, I am...

Perceiving with memory and
  associations
Seeing patterns and meanings
Seeing possibilities
Projecting possibilities for the future
Imagining; "reading between the lines"
Looking for the big picture
Having hunches; "ideas out of
  nowhere"
Letting "the mind tell the eyes"

T: THINKING JUDGMENT
When reasoning with thinking, I am...

Using logical analysis
Using objective and impersonal criteria
Drawing cause and effect relationships
Being firm-minded
Prizing logical order
Being skeptical

F: FEELING JUDGMENT
When reasoning with feeling, I am...

Applying personal priorities
Weighing human values and motives,
  my own and others
Appreciating
Valuing warmth in relationships
Prizing harmony; trusting

J: JUDGMENT
When I take a judging attitude, I am...

Using thinking or feeling judgment
  outwardly
Deciding and planning
Organizing and scheduling
Controlling and regulating
Goal oriented
Wanting closure, even when data are
  incomplete

P: PERCEPTION
When I take a perceiving attitude, I am...

Using sensing or intuitive perception
  outwardly
Taking in information
Adapting and changing
Curious and interested
Open-minded
Resisting closure to obtain more data

From *People Types and Tiger Stripes*, 3rd edition, copyright 1993 Gordon Lawrence

What the MBTI Reports

- The instrument you responded to, the Myers-Briggs Type Indicator ®
  (MBTI), identifies peoples' preferences among sets of mental processes.
- Each MBTI item you answered is counted on one of four scales.
- Each scale is made up of a pair of opposites, with a range between them
  and a midpoint, suggested by the diagram.
- Your answers on each scale add up to a preference score, to estimate how
  much you prefer one of each pair over the other. The larger your prefer-
  ence score, the farther it lies from the midpoint.
- The eight letters below represent preferred ways of attending to the world
  and making decisions, eight different mental habits.

```
E ——————————————|——————————————— I
S ——————————————|——————————————— N
T ——————————————|——————————————— F
J ——————————————|——————————————— P
```

- Everyone uses all eight, but each person has preferences among them and
  uses those more. It is a lot like handedness — everyone uses both hands,
  but favors and is better at using one of them.
- Each different combination of preferences represents a type — what the
  psychology pioneer Carl Jung called psychological types. There are 16
  combinations to represent the 16 types.
- A type is not a pigeonhole or stereotype; it is a particular way that mental
  energy is organized.
- Your results from the MBTI will indicate one of the 16 types descriptions
  for you to consider.

Descriptions of the Sixteen Types Reported by the MBTI

Using these descriptions and other resources, decide if the indicated description fits you. If it does, the resources will help you see many uses of
this knowledge. If the description does not seem to be a good fit, look for
another description that is a better fit. The person explaining your MBTI
results can direct you to the other resources. The MBTI is a tool to help
you start examining the types. While it was developed with great care, and
is accurate for most people, you are the one to decide which type is the
best fit for you. You may want to read all of the descriptions as you decide.

How to Read the Descriptions

The descriptions are grouped in two ways. The extraverting types are on the left page, introverting types on the right. The strongest mental process in each case is indicated by the larger letter in the four–letter type designation, such as ISFP.

The descriptions are arranged with opposite types across from each other, on the opposite pages; for example, ENTJ is across from ISFP, the type that is opposite in all four dimensions. As you read the phrases listed for each type, you should not assume that a positive value listed for one type implies a negative trait for the opposite type. For example, when we read that ENTJs value efficiency we must not infer that ISFPs are inefficient. Similarly, because ISFPs value compassion does not mean that ENTJs are cold-hearted. Opposite types are across from each other to help you decide your best fit type. The contrasts shown by the opposites help to clarify what is given priority in our mental processing. What has high priority for ISFP is not given high priority by ENTJ, and vice versa. The descriptions emphasize the values and priorities of the types more than they tell what behaviors are associated with each of the types. The values are emphasized because they are the motivation energy behind the behaviors.

ENTJ

Intuitive, innovative ORGANIZERS; analytical, systematic, confident; push to get action on new ideas and challenges. Having extraverted THINKING as their strongest mental process, ENTJs are at their best when they can take charge and set things in logical order. They value:

- Analyzing abstract problems, complex situations
- Foresight; pursuing a vision
- Changing, organizing things to fit their vision
- Putting theory into practice, ideas into action
- Working to a plan and schedule
- Initiating, then delegating
- Efficiency; removing obstacles and confusion
- Probing new possibilities
- Holding self and others to high standards
- Having things settled and closed
- Tough-mindedness, directness, task focus
- Objective principles; fairness, justice
- Assertive, direct action
- Intellectual resourcefulness
- Driving toward broad goals along a logical path
- Designing structures and strategies
- Seeking out logical flaws

ESTJ

Fact-minded practical ORGANIZERS; assertive, analytical, systematic; push to get things done and working smoothly and efficiently. Having extraverted THINKING as their strongest mental process, they are at their best when they can take charge and set things in logical order. They value:

- Results; doing, acting
- Planned, organized work and play
- Common sense practicality
- Consistency; standard procedures
- Concrete, present-day usefulness
- Deciding quickly and logically
- Having things settled and closed
- Rules, objective standards, fairness by the rules
- Task-focused behavior
- Directness, tough-mindedness
- Orderliness; no loose ends
- Systematic structure; efficiency
- Categorizing aspects of their life
- Scheduling and monitoring
- Protecting what works

ISFP

Observant, loyal HELPERS; reflective, realistic, empathic, patient with details. Shunning disagreements, they are gentle, reserved and modest. Having introverted FEELING as their strongest mental process, they are at their best when responding to needs of others. They value:

- Personal loyalty; a close, loyal friend
- Finding delight in the moment
- Seeing what needs doing to improve the moment
- Freedom from organizational constraints
- Working individually
- Peace-making behind the scenes
- Attentiveness to feelings
- Harmonious, cooperative work settings
- Spontaneous, hands-on exploration
- Gentle, respectful interactions
- Deeply-held personal beliefs
- Reserved, reflective behavior
- Practical, useful skills and know-how
- Having their work life be fully consistent with deeply-held values
- Showing and receiving appreciation

INFP

Imaginative, independent HELPERS; reflective, inquisitive, empathic, loyal to ideals: more tuned to possibilities than practicalities. Having introverted FEELING as their strongest mental process, they are at their best when their inner ideals find expression in their helping of people. They value:

- Harmony in the inner life of ideas
- Harmonious work settings; working individually
- Seeing the big picture possibilities
- Creativity; curiosity, exploring
- Helping people find their potential
- Giving ample time to reflect on decisions
- Adaptability and openness
- Compassion and caring; attention to feelings
- Work that lets them express their idealism
- Gentle, respectful interactions
- An inner compass; being unique
- Showing appreciation and being appreciated
- Ideas, language and writing
- A close, loyal friend
- Perfecting what is important

ESFJ

Practical HARMONIZERS, workers-with-people; sociable, orderly, opinioned; conscientious, realistic and well tuned to the here and now. Having extraverted FEELING as their strongest mental process, they are at their best when responsible for winning people's cooperation with personal caring and practical help. They value:

- An active, sociable life, with many relationships
- A concrete, present-day view of life
- Making daily routines into gracious living
- Staying closely tuned to people they care about so as to avoid interpersonal troubles
- Talking out problems cooperatively, caringly
- Approaching problems through rules, authority, standard procedures
- Caring, compassion and tactfulness
- Helping organizations serve their members well
- Responsiveness to others, and to traditions
- Being prepared, reliable in tangible, daily work
- Loyalty and faithfulness
- Practical skillfulness grounded in experience
- Structured learning in a humane setting

ENFJ

Imaginative HARMONIZERS, workers-with-people; expressive, orderly, opinioned, conscientious; curious about new ideas and possibilities. Having extraverted FEELING as their strongest mental process, they are at their best when responsible for winning people's cooperation with caring insight into their needs. They value:

- Having a wide circle of relationships
- Having a positive, enthusiastic view of life
- Seeing subtleties in people and interactions
- Understanding others' needs and concerns
- An active, energizing social life
- Seeing possibilities in people
- Thorough follow-through on important projects
- Working on several projects at once
- Caring and imaginative problem solving
- Maintaining relationships to make things work
- Shaping organizations to better serve members
- Sociability and responsiveness
- Structured learning in a humane setting
- Caring, compassion and tactfulness
- Appreciation as the natural means of encouraging improvements

INTP

Inquisitive ANALYZERS; reflective, independent, curious; more interested in organizing ideas than situations or people. Having introverted THINKING as their strongest mental process, they are at their best when following their intellectual curiosity, analyzing complexities to find the underlying logical principles. They value:

- A reserved outer life; inner life of logical inquiry
- Pursuing interests in depth, with concentration
- Work and play that is intriguing, not routine
- Being free of emotional issues when working
- Working on problems that respond to detached intuitive analysis and theorizing
- Approaching problems by reframing the obvious
- Complex intellectual mysteries
- Being absorbed in abstract, mental work
- Freedom from organizational constraints
- Independence and non-conformance
- Intellectual quickness, ingenuity, invention
- Competence in the world of ideas
- Spontaneous learning by following curiosity and inspirations

ISTP

Practical ANALYZERS; value exactness; more interested in organizing data than situations or people; reflective, cool and curious observers of life. Having introverted THINKING as their strongest mental process, they are at their best when analyzing experience to find the logical order and underlying properties of things. They value:

- A reserved outer life
- Having a concrete, present-day view of life
- Clear, exact facts; a large storehouse of them
- Looking for efficient, least-effort solutions based on experience
- Knowing how mechanical things work
- Pursuing interests in depth, such as hobbies
- Collecting things of interest
- Working on problems that respond to detached, sequential analysis and adaptability
- Freedom from organizational constraints
- Independence and self-management
- Spontaneous hands-on learning experience
- Having useful technical expertise
- Critical analysis as a means to improving things

ESTP

REALISTIC ADAPTERS in the world of material things; good natured, easy going; oriented to practical, first-hand experience; highly observant of details of things. Having extraverted SENSING as their strongest mental process, they are at their best when free to act on impulses, responding to concrete problems that need solving. They value:

- A life of outward, playful action, in the moment
- Being a trouble shooter
- Finding ways to use the existing system
- Clear, concrete, exact facts
- Knowing the way mechanical things work
- Being direct, to the point
- Learning through spontaneous, hands-on action
- Practical action, more than words
- Plunging into new adventures
- Responding to practical needs as they arise
- Seeing the expedient thing and acting on it
- Pursuing immediately useful skills
- Finding fun in their work and sparking others to have fun
- Looking for efficient, least-effort solutions
- Being caught up in enthusiasms

ESFP

REALISTIC ADAPTERS in human relationships; friendly and easy with people, highly observant of their feelings and needs; oriented to practical, first-hand experience. Extraverted SENSING being their strongest mental process, they are at their best when free to act on impulses, responding to needs of the here and now. They value:

- An energetic, sociable life, full of friends and fun
- Performing, entertaining, sharing
- Immediately useful skills; practical know-how
- Learning through spontaneous, hands-on action
- Trust and generosity; openness
- Patterning themselves after those they admire
- Concrete, practical knowledge; resourcefulness
- Caring, kindness, support, appreciation
- Freedom from irrelevant rules
- Handling immediate, practical problems, crises
- Seeing tangible realities; least-effort solutions
- Showing and receiving appreciation
- Making the most of the moment; adaptability
- Being caught up in enthusiasms
- Easing and brightening work and play

INFJ

People-oriented INNOVATORS of ideas; serious, quietly forceful and persevering; concerned with work that will help the world and inspire others. Having introverted INTUITION as their strongest mental process, they are at their best when caught up in inspiration, envisioning and creating ways to empower self and others to lead more meaningful lives. They value:

- A reserved outer life; spontaneous inner life
- Planning ways to help people improve
- Seeing complexities, hidden meanings
- Understanding others' needs and concerns
- Imaginative ways of saying things
- Planful, independent, academic learning
- Reading, writing, imagining; academic theories
- Being restrained in outward actions; planful
- Aligning their work with their ideals
- Pursuing and clarifying their ideals
- Taking the long view
- Bringing out the best in others through appreciation
- Finding harmonious solutions to problems
- Being inspired and inspiring others

INTJ

Logical, critical, decisive INNOVATORS of ideas; serious, intent, very independent, concerned with organization; determined, often stubborn. With introverted INTUITION as their strongest mental process, they are at their best when inspiration turns insights into ideas and plans for improving human knowledge and systems. They value:

- A restrained, organized outer life; a spontaneous, intuitive inner life
- Conceptual skills, theorizing
- Planful, independent, academic learning
- Skepticism; critical analysis; objective principles
- Originality, independence of mind
- Intellectual quickness, ingenuity
- Non-emotional tough-mindedness
- Freedom from interference in projects
- Working to a plan and schedule
- Seeing complexities, hidden meanings
- Improving things by finding flaws
- Probing new possibilities; taking the long view
- Pursuing a vision; foresight; conceptualizing
- Getting insights to reframe problems

ENTP

Inventive, analytical PLANNERS OF CHANGE; enthusiastic and independent; pursue inspiration with impulsive energy; seek to understand and inspire. Extraverted INTUITION being their strongest mental process, they are at their best when caught up in the enthusiasm of a new project and promoting its benefits. They value:

- Conceiving of new things and initiating change
- The surge of inspirations; the pull of emerging possibilities
- Analyzing complexities
- Following their insights, wherever they lead
- Finding meanings behind the facts
- Autonomy, elbow room, openness
- Ingenuity, originality, a fresh perspective
- Mental models and concepts that explain life
- Fair treatment
- Flexibility, adaptability
- Learning through action, variety and discovery
- Exploring theories and meanings behind events
- Improvising, looking for novel ways
- Work made light by inspiration

ENFP

Warmly enthusiastic PLANNERS OF CHANGE; imaginative, individualistic; pursue inspiration with impulsive energy; seek to understand and inspire others. With extraverted INTUITION as their strongest mental process, they are at their best when caught in the enthusiasm of a project, sparking others to see its benefits. They value:

- The surge of inspirations; the pull of emerging possibilities
- A life of variety, people, warm relationships
- Following their insights wherever they lead
- Finding meanings behind the facts
- Creativity, originality, a fresh perspective
- An optimistic, positive, enthusiastic view of life
- Flexibility and openness
- Exploring, devising and trying out new things
- Open ended opportunities and options
- Freedom from the requirement of being practical
- Learning through action, variety, and discovery
- A belief that any obstacle can be overcome
- A focus on people's potentials
- Brainstorming to solve problems
- Work made light and playful by inspiration

ISFJ

Sympathetic MANAGERS OF FACTS AND DETAILS, concerned with people's welfare; stable, conservative, dependable, painstaking, systematic. Having introverted SENSING as their strongest mental process, they are at their best when using their sensible intelligence and practical skills to help others in tangible ways. They value:

- Preserving, enjoying the things of proven value
- Steady, sequential work yielding reliable results
- A controlled, orderly outer life
- Patient, persistent attention to basic needs
- Following a sensible path, based on experience
- A rich memory for concrete facts
- Loyalty; strong relationships
- Consistency, familiarity, the tried and true
- First-hand experience of what is important
- Compassion, kindness, caring
- Working to a plan and schedule
- Learning through planned, sequential teaching
- Set routines, common sense options
- Rules, authority, set procedures
- Hard work, perseverance

ISTJ

Analytical MANAGER OF FACTS AND DETAILS; dependable, conservative, systematic, painstaking, decisive, stable. Having introverted SENSING as their strongest mental process, they are at their best when charged with organizing and maintaining data and material important to others and to themselves. They value:

- Steady, systematic work that yields reliable results
- A controlled outer life grounded in the present
- Following a sensible path, based on experience
- Concrete, exact, immediately useful facts, skills
- Consistency, familiarity, the tried and true
- A concrete, present-day view of life
- Working to a plan and schedule
- Preserving and enjoying things of proven value
- Proven systems, common sense options
- Freedom from emotionality in deciding things
- Learning through planned, sequential teaching
- Skepticism; wanting to read the fine print first
- A focus on hard work, perseverance
- Quiet, logical, detached problem solving
- Serious and focused work and play

Appendix 2
Additional Readings on Type and Teaching Composition

DiTiberio, John K. and George H. Jensen. *Writing & Personality: Finding Your Voice, Your Style, Your Way.* Palo Alto, CA: Davies-Black Publishing, 1995.

Gladis, Stephen. *Writetype: Personality Types and Writing Styles.* Amherst: Human Resources Development Press, 1993.

Harris, Muriel. "Don't Believe Everything You're Taught." *The Subject Is Writing.* Ed. Wendy Bishop. Portsmouth, NH: Boynton/Cook, 1993. 189–201.

Horning, Alice and Ron Sudol, Eds. *Understanding Literacy: Personality Preference in Rhetorical and Psycholinguistic Contexts.* Cresskill, NJ: Hampton Press, 1996.

Jensen, George H. "Learning Styles." *Applications of the Myers-Briggs Type Indicator in Higher Education.* Eds. Judith Provost and Scott Anchors. Palo Alto, CA: Consulting Psychologists Press, 1987. 181–206.

———. "The Reification of the Basic Writer." *Journal of Basic Writing* 5.1 (1986): 52–64.

Jensen, George H. and John K. DiTiberio. *Personality and the Teaching of Composition.* Norwood, NJ: Ablex, 1989.

Lawrence, Gordon. *People Type & Tiger Stripes,* 3rd ed. Gainesville, FL: Center for Applications of Psychological Type, 1993.

Maid, Barry, Sally Crisp, and Suzanne Norton. "On Gaining Insight into Ourselves as Writers and as Tutors: Our Use of the Myers-Briggs Type Indicator." *Writing Lab Newsletter* 13.10 (June 1989): 1–5.

Scharton, Maurice and Janice Neuleib. "The Gift of Insight: Personality Type, Tutoring, and Learning." *The Writing Center: New Directions.* Eds. Ray Wallace and Jeanne Simpson. New York: Garland, 1991. 184–203.

Thompson, Thomas C. "Personality Preferences, Tutoring Styles, and Implications for Tutor Training." *The Writing Center Journal* 14.2 (Spring 1994): 136–149.

Thompson, Thomas C. "Understanding Attitudes Toward Assessment: The Personality Factor." *Assessing Writing* 2.2 (1995): 191–206.

Contributors

Tom Thompson (ENFJ), a former high school teacher, currently teaches at The Citadel in Charleston, SC. His courses include first-year composition, advanced composition, public speaking, composition theory, responding to student writing, and personality theory and teaching English.

George H. Jensen (INTJ) teaches at Southwest Missouri State University. His courses include first-year composition, literary criticism, composition theory, modern rhetorical theory, and personality and writing. His publications include *Personality and the Teaching of Composition* and *Writing and Personality* (both co-authored with John K. DiTiberio).

Dean A. Hinnen (ESTP), a former newspaper reporter and editor, is a doctoral candidate in English (rhetoric and composition) at Texas Christian University. He has taught freshman and sophomore composition, served for a year as acting director of the Writing Center at Southwest Missouri State University, and for a year as associate director of composition at Texas Christian University.

Barry Maid (ENTP) teaches at the University of Arkansas at Little Rock. He teaches courses in technical writing, computers (including the Internet) and writing, and personality and writing.

Maurice Scharton (ENTP) teaches writing and rhetoric at Illinois State University and pursues a research interest in tests of writing ability. His text, *Inside/Out: A Guide to Writing* (co-authored with Janice Neuleib), implements type theory for writing instruction.

Janice Neuleib (INTJ) is a professor at Illinois State University where she teaches composition theory, instructional theory and research, and stylistics. She has written on type theory and practice in *Inside/Out: A Guide to Writing* (co-authored with Maurice Scharton).

Alice Horning (ISTJ) teaches Rhetoric and Linguistics at Oakland University in Rochester, Michigan. Another of her essays on the relationship of personality and writing appears in *Understanding Literacy: Personality Preferences in Rhetorical and Psycholinguistic Contexts* (co-edited with Ron Sudol).

Jane Bowman Smith (INFJ) teaches at Winthrop University in Rock Hill, SC. She is presently co-editing a book on student self-assessment and teaches freshman composition, advanced composition, rhetorical theory, the teaching of writing in the public schools, and writing center theory.

Muriel Harris (ESFJ) is a professor of English and Director of the Writing Lab at Purdue University. She edits the *Writing Lab Newsletter* and wrote *Teaching One-to-One: The Writing Conference, Prentice Hall Reference Guide to Grammar and Usage* (now in the third edition), and book chapters and journal articles on writing center theory and practice, individualized instruction in writing, and OWLs (Online Writing Labs).

Ronald A. Sudol (INTJ) is Professor of Rhetoric at Oakland University, where he teaches composition, public rhetoric, media criticism, and American studies. He is co-editor (with Alice Horning) of the collection of essays *Understanding Literacy: Personality Preference in Rhetorical and Psycholinguistic Contexts*.

Vicki Collins (ENTJ) teaches in the English Department at Oregon State University, where she also directs the university's Writing Intensive Curriculum and leads seminars for faculty on teaching with writing. Her courses include Writing for Teachers, Writing Across the Disciplines, and literature and poetry courses.